LIBRARY
NSCC, WATERFRONT CAMPUS
80 MAWIO'MI PLACE
DARTMOUTH, NS  B2Y 0A5 CANADA

QH
442
.2
C5645
2006

# CLONING

Other books in the Introducing Issues
with Opposing Viewpoints series:

AIDS
Alcohol
Civil Liberties
The Death Penalty
Gangs
Gay Marriage
Genetic Engineering
Smoking
Terrorism

INTRODUCING ISSUES WITH

OPPOSING VIEWPOINTS®

# CLONING

Louise I. Gerdes, *Book Editor*

Bruce Glassman, *Vice President*
Bonnie Szumski, *Publisher, Series Editor*
Helen Cothran, *Managing Editor*

OPPOSING VIEWPOINTS® SERIES

**GREENHAVEN PRESS**
*An imprint of Thomson Gale, a part of The Thomson Corporation*

THOMSON

GALE

Detroit • New York • San Francisco • San Diego • New Haven, Conn. • Waterville, Maine • London • Munich

© 2006 Thomson Gale, a part of The Thomson Corporation.

Thomson and Star Logo are trademarks and Gale and Greenhaven Press are registered trademarks used herein under license.

*For more information, contact*
Greenhaven Press
27500 Drake Rd.
Farmington Hills, MI 48331-3535
Or you can visit our Internet site at http://www.gale.com

**ALL RIGHTS RESERVED.**
No part of this work covered by the copyright hereon may be reproduced or used in any form or by any means—graphic, electronic, or mechanical, including photocopying, recording, taping, Web distribution or information storage retrieval systems—without the written permission of the publisher.

Every effort has been made to trace the owners of copyrighted material.

**LIBRARY OF CONGRESS CATALOGING-IN-PUBLICATION DATA**

Cloning / Louise I. Gerdes, book editor.
   p. cm. — (Introducing issues with opposing viewpoints)
  Includes bibliographical references and index.
  ISBN 0-7377-3220-2 (lib : alk. paper)
  1. Cloning—Social aspects. I. Gerdes, Louise I., 1953– II. Series.
  QH442.2.C5645 2006
  176—dc22

                        2005046292

Printed in the United States of America

# CONTENTS

Indulging in a wide spectrum of ideas, beliefs, and perspectives is a critical cornerstone of democracy. After all, it is often debates over differences of opinion, such as whether to legalize abortion, how to treat prisoners, or when to enact the death penalty, that shape our society and drive it forward. Such diversity of thought is frequently regarded as the hallmark of a healthy and civilized culture. As the Reverend Clifford Schutjer of the First Congregational Church in Mansfield, Ohio, declared in a 2001 sermon, "Surrounding oneself with only like-minded people, restricting what we listen to or read only to what we find agreeable is irresponsible. Refusing to entertain doubts once we make up our minds is a subtle but deadly form of arrogance." With this advice in mind, Introducing Issues with Opposing Viewpoints books aim to open readers' minds to the critically divergent views that comprise our world's most important debates.

Introducing Issues with Opposing Viewpoints simplifies for students the enormous and often overwhelming mass of material now available via print and electronic media. Collected in every volume is an array of opinions that capture the essence of a particular controversy or topic. Introducing Issues with Opposing Viewpoints books embody the spirit of nineteenth-century journalist Charles A. Dana's axiom: "Fight for your opinions, but do not believe that they contain the whole truth, or the only truth." Absorbing such contrasting opinions teaches students to analyze the strength of an argument and compare it to its opposition. From this process readers can inform and strengthen their own opinions, or be exposed to new information that will change their minds. Introducing Issues with Opposing Viewpoints is a mosaic of different voices. The authors are statesmen, pundits, academics, journalists, corporations, and ordinary people who have felt compelled to share their experiences and ideas in a public forum. Their words have been collected from newspapers, journals, books, speeches, interviews, and the Internet, the fastest growing body of opinionated material in the world.

Introducing Issues with Opposing Viewpoints shares many of the well-known features of its critically acclaimed parent series, Opposing Viewpoints. The articles are presented in a pro/con format, allowing readers to absorb divergent perspectives side by side. Active reading questions preface each viewpoint, requiring the student to approach the material thoughtfully and carefully. Useful charts, graphs, and cartoons supplement each article. A thorough introduction provides readers with crucial background on an issue. An annotated bibliography points the reader toward articles, books, and Web sites that contain additional information on the topic. An appendix of organizations to contact contains a wide variety of charities, nonprofit organizations, political groups, and private enterprises that each hold a position on the issue at hand. Finally, a comprehensive index allows readers to locate content quickly and efficiently.

Introducing Issues with Opposing Viewpoints is also significantly different from Opposing Viewpoints. As the series title implies, its presentation will help introduce students to the concept of opposing viewpoints, and learn to use this material to aid in critical writing and debate. The series' four-color, accessible format makes the books attractive and inviting to readers of all levels. In addition, each viewpoint has been carefully edited to maximize a reader's understanding of the content. Short but thorough viewpoints capture the essence of an argument. A substantial, thought-provoking essay question placed at the end of each viewpoint asks the student to further investigate the issues raised in the viewpoint, compare and contrast two authors' arguments, or consider how one might go about forming an opinion on the topic at hand. Each viewpoint contains sidebars that include at-a-glance information and handy statistics. A Facts About section located in the back of the book further supplies students with relevant facts and figures.

Following in the tradition of the Opposing Viewpoints series, Greenhaven Press continues to provide readers with invaluable exposure to the controversial issues that shape our world. As John Stuart Mill once wrote: "The only way in which a human being can make some approach to knowing the whole of a subject is by hearing what can be said about it by persons of every variety of opinion and studying all modes in which it can be looked at by every character of mind. No wise man ever acquired his wisdom in any mode but this." It is to this principle that Introducing Issues with Opposing Viewpoints books are dedicated.

# INTRODUCTION

*"Creating human embryos for research . . . creates a caste of humans only to serve the needs of others."*
— David Prentice, senior fellow at the Family Research Council

*"Banning all forms of cloning would slam the door on hope for up to 100 million Americans."*
— Daniel Perry, president of the Coalition for the Advancement of Medical Research

While some people view therapeutic cloning as a miraculous process that could help millions who suffer from debilitating diseases such as Alzheimer's, diabetes, and Parkinson's, others see it as immoral, the equivalent of playing God. People on both sides of the cloning debate have strong opinions about cloning that are

*South Korean scientist Hwang Woo-Suk and U.S. scientist Gerald Schatten, two of the world's leading cloning researchers, discuss recent advances in therapeutic cloning technology with members of the press.*

often shaped by their understanding of the process. People's conception of cloning can come from a variety of sources, and each source may describe or portray the process quite differently.

Some people learn about cloning from public policy organizations that promote traditional values. Organizations such as Concerned Women of America, the Family Research Council, and the Traditional Values Coalition oppose cloning because they believe that cloning results in the creation of a human being. Cloning human egg cells simply to destroy them for medical research, for example, is abhorrent. These organizations believe, "The embryo, however created and however small, is a human being and therefore should be granted the rights and protections of a human being," asserts law and medical

*A blastocyst multiplies in this magnified image. A blastocyst is a cluster of human cells created by inserting DNA into an unfertilized human egg.*

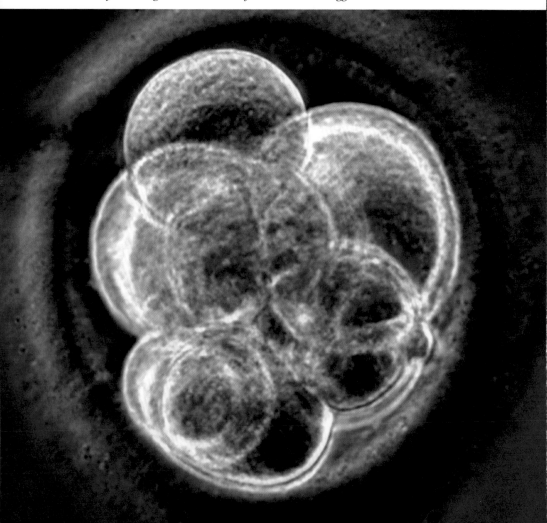

ethics professor R. Alto Charo. In order to advance their point of view, activists from these organizations often depict cloning to emphasize that the process creates and destroys human life. Family Research Council representative David Prentice, for example, describes cloning in the following way:

> The chromosomes of an egg cell are replaced with the nucleus of a somatic (body) cell. If the resulting embryo is then inserted into a womb in hopes of a live birth, it is called "reproductive cloning." If the embryo is destroyed to harvest its stem cells for experiments, it is called "therapeutic cloning." But these are not two separate types of cloning: The same embryo—produced by the same technique—is the starting point for both uses.

By using the word *embryo* to describe the cloned cell, Prentice underscores the council's belief that the cell is a human being. He also argues that the two cloning processes are indistinguishable—both produce an embryo. The goal of implanting the embryo in the womb is to produce a cloned human baby, asserts Prentice. The goal of therapeutic cloning is to sacrifice the embryo for purposes of medical experimentation, he claims. Such descriptions inspire a negative image of both reproductive and therapeutic cloning.

Others learn about therapeutic cloning from organizations that advocate for the advancement of science and medicine. While the American Medical Association, the Center for American Progress, and the Coalition for the Advancement of Medical Research oppose reproductive cloning, they approve of therapeutic cloning. In their view therapeutic cloning provides hope for those suffering from paralyzing injuries and debilitating diseases. Organization advocates use scientific language to describe the process and distinguish between reproductive and therapeutic cloning. Daniel Perry, president of the Coalition for the Advancement of Medical Research, thus describes the therapeutic cloning process quite differently from Prentice:

> Therapeutic cloning, or somatic cell nuclear transfer technology (SCNT) . . . is fundamentally different [from reproductive cloning]. SCNT involves removing the nucleus of a skin, heart, nerve or any other non-germ cell, then stimulating this cell to

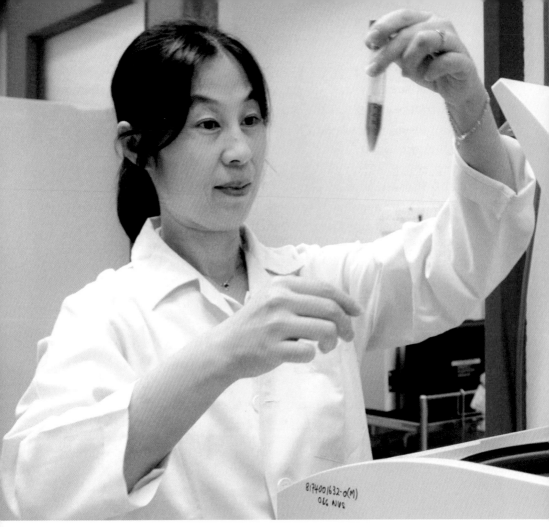

*Although many object to the idea of reproductive cloning, researchers such as this woman working at a laboratory in Singapore are excited by its potential.*

begin dividing. It is important to remember that this tiny batch of cells—smaller than the period at the end of this sentence— never leaves the lab, nor is it transplanted into a womb. No sperm is used. Instead, researchers store the unfertilized egg cells in a lab, where they are used to produce stem cells.

Perry does not refer to the cloned egg as an embryo but as a tiny batch of cells that is created in a lab where it will be used only for medical research. He contends that the creation of the cloned cell is in no way connected to the process of human reproduction. Descriptions such as these paint a positive picture of therapeutic cloning, a process that advances medical science.

Patient groups are another source of information about therapeutic cloning. These groups, which include both patients and family members, represent the interests of those who suffer from debilitating injuries or degenerative diseases. "They are the ones who can put human faces on the debate and can describe the health-care benefit," claims biotech industry spokesperson Michael Werner. Celebrity

*Former first lady Nancy Reagan supports therapeutic cloning to treat debilitating diseases such as Alzheimer's.*

*Scientist Hwang Woo-Suk, who cloned the first human embryo, claims that restricting stem cell research impedes progress toward medical breakthroughs.*

patients and family members can be particularly influential. Actor Christopher Reeve, for example, famous for his role as Superman, was a leading advocate of therapeutic cloning. Reeve, who was left paralyzed after a fall from a horse, believed that therapeutic cloning would ultimately lead to a cure for spinal chord injuries such as his. Former first lady Nancy Reagan is another well-known advocate of therapeutic cloning. She believes that therapeutic cloning offers hope to those suffering from Alzheimer's, the debilitating disease that struck her husband, former president Ronald Reagan. Celebrity advocates such as Christopher Reeve and Nancy Reagan arouse an optimistic view of therapeutic cloning.

Noncelebrity patient advocates can also be passionate sources of information about therapeutic cloning. Many parents can empathize with the parents of children who suffer from paralyzing injuries and degenerative diseases. Thus Don C. Reed, the father of a paralyzed child, might for some be a persuasive source on cloning. Reed writes:

> My son Roman Reed is paralyzed, and every day he suffers the agonies of the damned. . . .When the day comes that my son gets his operation, it will begin with a q-tip swabbing the inside of his mouth. Those gathered cells will be microscopically injected into a donated egg, like a woman loses every month. After five days, stem cells will be taken from that hollowed egg. They will never be allowed to grow, or develop: only multiply. When there are enough (several million, like half a cup of water with nearly invisible specks) it will be placed inside Roman's injured neck. There, we hope, the cells will become the new and healthy nerves he needs, reconnecting body and brain.

Ardent appeals such as Reed's, which depict cloning as a life-saving procedure, further a hopeful vision of cloning.

People on both sides of the therapeutic cloning debate continue to shape how others perceive the cloning process. The authors in this anthology describe their own visions of cloning in the following chapters of *Introducing Issues with Opposing Viewpoints: Cloning:* Should Reproductive Cloning Be Pursued? Should Therapeutic Cloning Be Pursued? Should Animal Cloning Be Pursued?

# CHAPTER 1

# Should Reproductive Cloning Be Pursued?

# Reproductive Cloning Is Ethical

**Gregory E. Pence**

*"The origins of a person . . . do not affect [its] personhood. . . . The same would be true of a child created by cloning."*

Reproductive cloning is not unethical, argues Gregory E. Pence in the following viewpoint. Claims that soulless clones will be created for selfish, immoral reasons are unfounded, he argues. Clones would be no different from children created sexually, he maintains. In fact, he asserts, because cloning gives infertile couples the opportunity to have biologically related children, clones are more likely to be loved than many children created by sexual reproduction. Moreover, once born, clones would be entitled to the same human rights as any human being, Pence contends. Pence, a philosophy and medical ethics professor at the University of Alabama at Birmingham, is author of *Who's Afraid of Human Cloning?*

**AS YOU READ, CONSIDER THE FOLLOWING QUESTIONS:**

1. Under what conditions does Pence think that cloning might be a constitutionally protected right?
2. To what specific rights does the author claim a clone will be entitled?
3. Does the author believe that the government has the right to judge a couple's reason for having a child?

Gregory E. Pence, "The Top Ten Myths About Human Cloning," www.humancloning.org, 2001. Copyright © 2001 by Gregory E. Pence. Reproduced by permission.

### Human Cloning Is Replication or Making Children into Commodities

Opponents of cloning often use these words to beg the question, to assume that children created by parents by a new method would not be loved. Similar things were said about "test tube" babies, who turned out to be some of the most-wanted, most-loved babies ever created in human history.

Indeed, the opposite is true: evolution has created us with sex drives such that, if we do not carefully use contraception, children occur. Because children get created this way without being wanted, sexual reproduction is more likely to create unwanted, and hence possibly unloved, children than human cloning.

*The Korean scientists (pictured) who cloned the first human embryo hope that embryonic stem cells will lead to cures for debilitating diseases.*

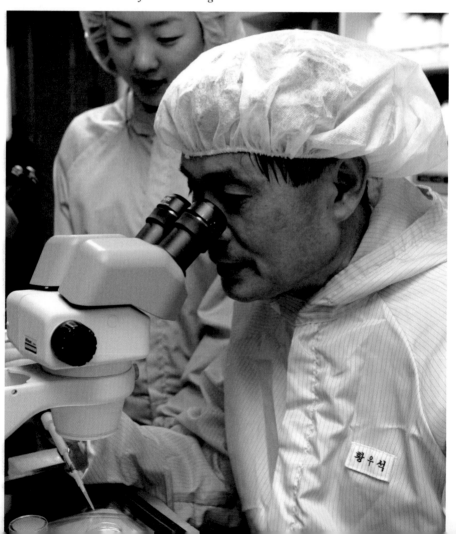

Lawyers opposing cloning have a special reason for using these pejorative words. If cloning is just a new form of human reproduction, then it is Constitutionally protected from interference by the state. Several Supreme Court decisions declare that all forms of human reproduction, including the right not to reproduce, cannot be abridged by government.

## People Created by Cloning Would Be Less Ensouled than Normal Humans, or Would Be Sub-Human

A human who had the same number of chromosomes as a child created sexually, who was gestated by a woman, and who talked, felt, and spoke as any other human, would ethically be human and a person. It is by now a principle of ethics that the origins of a person, be it from mixed-race parents, unmarried parents, in vitro fertilization, or a gay male couple hiring a surrogate mother, do not affect the personhood of the child born. The same would be true of a child created by cloning (who, of course, has to be gestated for nine months by a woman).

Every deviation from normal reproduction has always been faced with this fear. Children greeted by sperm donation, in vitro fertilization, and surrogate motherhood were predicted to be less-than-human, but were not.

A variation predicts that while, in fact, they will not be less-than-human, people will treat them this way and hence, such children will be harmed. This objection reifies prejudice and makes it an ethical justification, which it is wrong to do. The correct response to prejudice is to expose it for what it is, combat it with reason and with evidence, not validate it as an ethical reason.

> ## FAST FACT
>
> A common misconception is that a human clone, if created, would magically appear at the same age as the original. Cloning is an alternative way to create an embryo, not a full-grown individual. The cloned embryo, once created, must develop exactly the same way traditionally fertilized embryos do, in the womb. The baby clone would grow up having its own unique experiences and would therefore never be an exact duplicate.

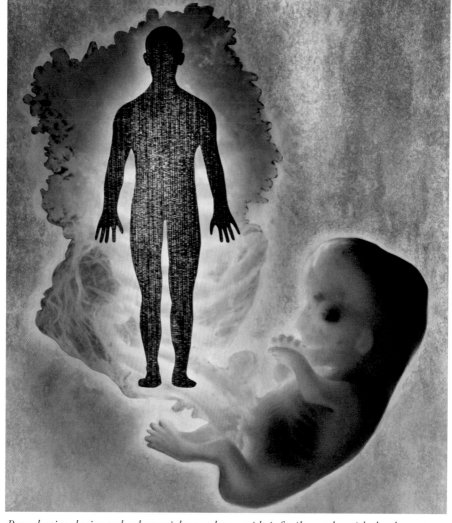

*Reproductive cloning technology might one day provide infertile couples with the chance to have a biologically related child.*

## People Created by Cloning Could Be Used for Spare Organs for Normal Humans

Nothing could be done to a person created by cloning that right now could not be done to your brother or to a person's twin. The U.S. Constitution strongly implies that once a human fetus is outside the womb and alive, he has rights. Decisions backing this up give him rights to inherit property, rights not to suffer discrimination because of disability, and rights to U.S. citizenship.

A variation of this myth assumes that a dictator could make cloned humans into special SWAT teams or suicidal bombers. But nothing about originating people this way gives anyone any special power over the resulting humans, who would have free will. Besides, if a dictator wants to create such assassins, he need not wait for cloning but can take orphans and try to indoctrinate them now in isolated camps.

**Only Selfish People Want to Create a Child by Cloning**
First, this assumes that ordinary people don't create children for selfish reasons, such as a desire to have someone take care of them in old age, a desire to see part of themselves continue after death, and/or the desire to leave their estate to someone. Many people are hypocritical or deceived about why they came to have children. Very few people just decide that they want to bring more joy into the world, and hence create a child to raise and support for life as an end-in-himself. Let's be honest here. Second, a couple using cloning need not create a copy of one of them. . . .

*Advocates of reproductive cloning maintain that cloning offers parents an alternative way to start a family.*

On the other hand, if a couple chooses a famous person, critics accuse them of creating designer babies. Either way, they can't win: if they re-create one of their genotypes, they are narcissistic; if they choose someone else's genes, they're guilty of creating designer babies.

In general, why should a couple using cloning have a higher justification required of them than a couple using sexual reproduction? If we ask: what counts as a good reason for creating a child, then why should cloning have any special test that is not required for sexual reproduction? Indeed, and more generally, what right does government have to require, or judge, any couple's reasons for having a child, even if they are seen by others to be selfish?

Couples desiring to use cloning should not bear an undue burden of justification.

### Human Cloning Is Inherently Evil: It Can Only Be Used for Bad Purposes by Bad People

No, it's just a tool, just another way to create a family. A long legacy in science fiction novels and movies make the word "cloning" so fraught with bad connotations that it can hardly be used in any discussion that purports to be impartial. It is like discussing equal rights for women by starting to discuss whether "the chicks" would fare better with equal rights. To most people, "cloning" implies selfish parents, crazy scientists, and out-of-control technology, so a fair discussion using this word isn't possible. Perhaps the phrase, "somatic cell nuclear transplantation" is better, even if it's a scientific mouthful. So if we shouldn't call a person created by cloning, a "clone," what should we call him? Answer: a person.

> ### EVALUATING THE AUTHOR'S ARGUMENTS:
>
> In the viewpoint you just read, Gregory E. Pence equates reproductive cloning with sexual reproduction to support his claims. Is this comparison necessary to support his arguments? Explain why or why not.

# Reproductive Cloning Is Unethical

## Peter J. Cataldo

*"Human cloning in any form is a serious offence against human dignity."*

An embryo is a human being, asserts Peter J. Cataldo in the following viewpoint excerpted from testimony given before the Massachusetts Senate Committee on Science and Technology. Cloning an embryo to exploit its therapeutic or reproductive potential, he argues, is therefore unethical. Claims that therapeutic cloning, the cloning of embryonic stem cells to cure diseases, is different from reproductive cloning, the cloning of whole human beings, are unsound, Cataldo argues. The embryo has the potential to become a human being, he contends; thus the argument that embryos used in therapeutic cloning are not yet human beings is irrelevant. Cataldo is director of research at the National Catholic Bioethics Center in Brighton, Massachusetts.

AS YOU READ, CONSIDER THE FOLLOWING QUESTIONS:
1. According to Cataldo, why is the teaching of the Roman Catholic Church appropriate in a discussion of cloning?
2. In the author's opinion, why does it make no difference that 50–80 percent of embryos in natural gestation never implant and die?
3. What does human cloning in any form represent, in the author's view?

Peter J. Cataldo, testimony before the Massachusetts Senate Committee on Science and Technology, December 12, 2001.

I would like to present some of the reasons why the Roman Catholic Church teaches that human cloning in any form is a serious offence against human dignity and should be prohibited. As a preface to my remarks, it is important to understand that the teaching of the Church on this subject is not any less credible because it originates from a religious body. Rather, the Church's teaching respects and defers to the findings of science and incorporates the natural moral law, which is open and applicable to all. Indeed, Catholics are held to believe the Church's teaching in these matters in part because of these two universal sources of human knowledge and action.

## Cloning Human Beings

The question of cloning "whole human beings" in reproductive cloning, as distinct from therapeutic cloning, is a distinction without a difference from a moral point of view. The particular future of an embryo does not make a difference to its status as a human being. In both therapeutic and reproductive cloning a human being is engendered who is a legitimate bearer of human rights. The fact that in one case and not in the other the embryo is allowed to progress into later stages of development, or that an estimated 50–80% of embryos in natural gestation never implant and die, or that the embryo prevented from implanting is destined to die, do not make an essential difference to whether the embryo is, *per se*, a human being.

These are all circumstances which are extraneous to what it means to be an actual human being. If an embryo possesses the complete human genome and has an intrinsic unity in which all of its parts act for the integral good of the whole, then it exists as a human being, and not as a formless, aimless "ball of cells," nor as mere "cellular life." Moreover, the fact that the cells of the early embryo are not yet differentiated [have not yet developed to their specific function], but are totipotent [able to develop into unlike cells or a new organism] and can become another embryo if separated, does not alter the reality that at any given point in its development the embryo functions as one unified organism. The early embryo is only potentially, not actually, divisible into another embryo. It is actually one, unified being with a human nature. The human embryo, in other words, is a human being.

This fact is a sufficient basis upon which to treat the embryo as a subject of fundamental human rights which the Catholic Church has consistently maintained. "Human embryos obtained *in vitro*," the Church teaches, "are human beings and subjects with rights: their dignity and right to life must be respected from the first moment of their existence. *"It is immoral to produce human embryos destined to be exploited as disposable 'biological material'* (Congregation for the Doctrine of the Faith, *Instruction on Respect for Human Life in its Origin and on the Dignity of Procreation* I, 5)." Human cloning in

*The newly elected pope, Benedict XVI, considers all forms of cloning to be immoral.*

WE'RE FINALLY PUTTING IT ALL TOGETHER!

HUMAN CLONING

Source: Siers. © 2001 by *The Charlotte Observer.* Reproduced by permission.

any form represents the ultimate domination over, and manipulation of, some human beings by others. But this conclusion is not the end of the story, because the Church embraces science at its core, and encourages any means to cure or ameliorate disease which respects human dignity, including the proven and promising alternatives of adult and cord blood stem cell research.

## EVALUATING THE AUTHOR'S ARGUMENTS:

In the viewpoint you just read, in order to overcome objections by those who claim that a religious perspective is not appropriate in the cloning debate, Peter J. Cataldo begins by explaining that the Roman Catholic Church respects scientific findings. Can you identify in the viewpoint any sentences or phrases that are critical of science? Does this make his viewpoint more or less persuasive? Explain.

**VIEWPOINT**

**3**

# Reproductive Cloning Should Be Banned

**Alan Trounson**

*"Reproductive cloning of humans should be off limits everywhere."*

Reproductive cloning is a crime against humanity and must be banned, argues Alan Trounson in the following viewpoint. Animal cloning experiments have proven that cloning is dangerous; thus world leaders must take a stand against those who plan to take the same risks with human beings, Trounson claims. Human cloning, like Nazi experiments conducted on concentration camp prisoners, should officially be named a crime against humanity, sending a clear message to those who pursue human cloning that they will be punished, he maintains. Professor Trounson is director of the Institute of Reproduction and Development at Monash University in Melbourne, Australia.

**AS YOU READ, CONSIDER THE FOLLOWING QUESTIONS:**
1. According to Trounson, why is the United Nations not sending the message that reproductive cloning is dangerous?
2. What is the difference between reproductive cloning and therapeutic cloning, in the author's opinion?
3. What do some fear will happen if reproductive cloning is placed in the same moral bracket as war crimes, in the author's view?

Alan Trounson, "A Crime Against Humanity," *New Scientist*, vol. 180, November 22–28, 2003, p. 23.
Copyright © 2003 by Reed Elsevier Business Publishing, Ltd. Reproduced by permission.

S ooner or later someone with the necessary skills and resources will be attracted by money or fame to demonstrate that reproductive cloning is feasible. Seven years after Dolly the sheep, would-be baby cloners have become a real worry. The international community, through the UN [United Nations], should be sending out the clearest possible signal about the dangers of reproductive cloning.

## Two Types of Cloning

Yet that message is not being sent. The sticking point is that some countries, notably the US and the Vatican, want a global ban on both therapeutic and reproductive cloning, while others want to ban only reproductive cloning. While the impasse continues, the UN appears weak and divided on the issue.

*This microscopic photo illustrates how cloning procedures are carried out, as a somatic cell is injected into an enucleated human egg cell.*

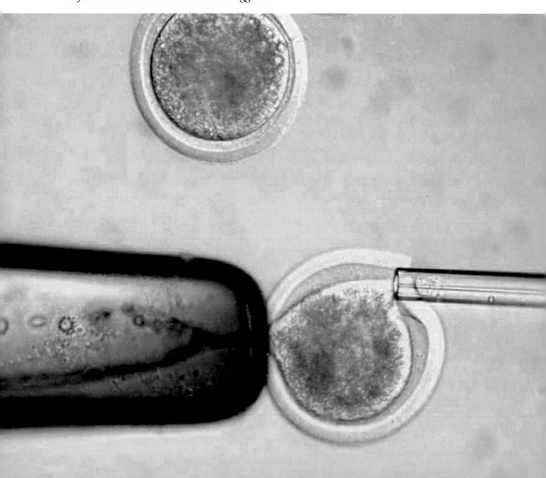

So what is the way forward? . . . As a cell biologist and a researcher in stem cell medicine I have glimpsed for myself the medical potential of nuclear transfer. This, the core technique used in creating Dolly, involves stripping an egg of its own genetic material and using it to "reprogram" an adult cell so it can begin the developmental process all over again.

It may turn out that therapeutic cloning will prove unsustainable as a method for producing tissues for grafting into patients, because of the need to access large numbers of human eggs. But even then, our only chance of discovering alternative methods of generating stem cells suitable for grafting will be to investigate the genetic reprogramming that takes place inside eggs during the early stages of the cloning process. The governments pressing for a global ban on therapeutic cloning are in my view misguided: each country should be free to set its own laws on this research.

Reproductive cloning is an entirely different matter. In recent years we have seen a crop of papers from animal cloners cataloguing the health risks involved. In light of these, the overwhelming majority of experts worldwide, myself included, believe that reproductive cloning of humans should be off limits everywhere. The question is how this can best be achieved, given the . . . impasse at the UN.

## A Crime Against Humanity

The approach that I, along with many of my colleagues, advocate is to make reproductive cloning a crime against humanity. We have lent our support to an organisation called the Genetics Policy Institute (GPI), which . . . submitted legal documents that state the case for classifying reproductive cloning as a crime against humanity.

> # FAST FACT
>
> **Nearly all countries agree that reproductive cloning, or the creation of an identical human being through asexual reproductive methods, should be banned. As of July 2004, however, only 30 of the 191 states recognized by the United Nations, including Britain, Belgium, Canada, Denmark, Germany, the Netherlands, and Spain, have outlawed reproductive cloning. The United States has not yet passed a law banning reproductive cloning, but several states such as California have done so.**

The GPI is calling on the UN to seek a ruling on the matter from the International Court of Justice.

A number of legal grounds can be cited in favour of such a declaration. For instance, the famous Nuremberg code of ethics, drafted in 1947 following the horrific experiments carried out by the Nazis in concentration camps, states: "No experiment should be conducted where there is a prior reason to believe that a death or disabling injury will

*Some compare reproductive cloning to the horrific human experiments carried out in Nazi concentration camps, crimes for which many Nazis were tried before an international tribunal in Nuremberg (pictured).*

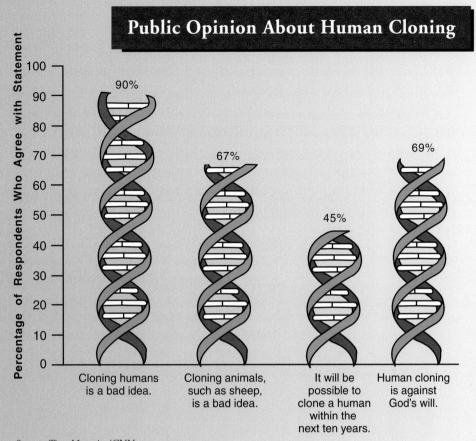

## Public Opinion About Human Cloning

Percentage of Respondents Who Agree with Statement

- 90% — Cloning humans is a bad idea.
- 67% — Cloning animals, such as sheep, is a bad idea.
- 45% — It will be possible to clone a human within the next ten years.
- 69% — Human cloning is against God's will.

Source: *Time Magazine*/CNN.

occur." The code also states that "the degree of risk to be taken should never exceed that determined by the humanitarian importance of the problem to be solved in the experiment".

Some may consider this proposal disproportionate or even draconian [exceedingly harsh]. But the fact is that plain moral outrage has so far failed to stop the posturing of the baby cloners, and it is clearly risky to continue to rely on the inefficiency of cloning as the main barrier to it being done. The outcome of animal experiments suggests that it will probably take 300 or more human eggs to obtain a single cloned pregnancy. If 20 or 30 women were sufficiently well paid, they might well donate the required number of eggs.

Others might worry that placing reproductive cloning in the same moral bracket as terrible war crimes risks devaluing the term "crime against humanity". They should remember that reproductive cloning itself is likely to have terrible consequences. Judging from the biology of animal clones, any fetus produced is likely to be abnormal and fail to develop to term. And any babies that do go to term and survive birth would face the prospect of living with some potential life-threatening abnormality. And for what purpose?

There are only three reasons for attempting to clone someone: narcissism [self-centeredness], infamy, or the misguided belief that it can be used to treat sterility. The entire scientific community should join the GPI in calling for it to be banned. A clear line needs to be drawn between reproductive cloning and the genuine investigation of medical benefits of other studies on nuclear transfer. Time is running out.

## EVALUATING THE AUTHOR'S ARGUMENTS:

In the viewpoint you just read, Alan Trounson claims that there are only three reasons for attempting to clone a human being: narcissism, infamy, or to treat sterility. Why do you think he makes this claim? Does it make his argument more or less persuasive? Explain.

# Reproductive Cloning Should Be Regulated, Not Banned

*Economist*

*"An indefinite ban on cloning research could have worse consequences than careful regulation."*

In the following viewpoint the editors of the British newsmagazine the *Economist* contend that regulating human cloning is a better way to control cloning than banning it. Regulating human cloning would subject the process to rigorous controls and subject those who violate the rules to penalties, they claim. Moreover, since people worldwide disagree about human cloning, enacting complete bans makes it difficult for nations to agree on how best to control it, the authors maintain. In addition, they argue, a complete ban on human cloning will not prevent people who desperately want children from seeking out potentially unscrupulous people to help them have a cloned child.

## AS YOU READ, CONSIDER THE FOLLOWING QUESTIONS:

1. In the authors' opinion, why is it currently foolhardy to pursue cloning experiments on humans?
2. According to the authors, what are some of the reasons people want to clone?
3. What do the authors claim should be the goal of cloning policy?

*Economist*, "How Far to Go," January 2, 2003. Copyright © 2003 by The Economist Newspaper Ltd., www.economist.com. All rights reserved. Reproduced by permission.

S ince Dolly the cloned sheep made her public debut in 1997, human cloning has been more a question of "when" than of "if". Yet for almost six years, legislators in most countries have done little to regulate this area of science. Britain is one of a mere 20 or so countries that ban reproductive cloning. Attempts at the United Nations [UN] to draw up an international treaty regulating human reproductive cloning have gone nowhere. This lost opportunity is lamentable. International bans take years to implement, even against evils such as biological weapons. Agreement on reproductive cloning will be harder still, given that most of those who demand it are bent not on world destruction, but on personal happiness—overcoming infertility or assuaging the loss of a previous child.

## FAST FACT

On December 27, 2002, chemist Bridgette Boisselier announced that she and fellow Clonaid scientists had created the first human clone, a baby girl she called Eve. Boisselier, a bishop of a religious group called the Raelians, who believe that aliens populated the earth twenty-five thousand years ago by cloning themselves, offered no scientific data to back up her claims. Clonaid, an organization devoted to promoting reproductive human cloning, has refused offers from leading U.S. scientists to perform tests on the mother and infant that would confirm whether Eve is in fact a clone.

## The Arguments Against Human Cloning

Plenty of people see a simple answer: ban cloning. America hopes to stop research not just on reproductive cloning but on the therapeutic cloning of embryos, created as a source of stem cells and destroyed within 14 days.[1]

Certainly from a medical perspective, reproductive cloning is fraught with risk. For every healthy animal cloned, many die along the way, and others suffer complications in later life. Scientists do not know what accounts for all these animal casualties, and until they do, it would be foolhardy to pursue experiments in humans.

As for ethics, some objectors dislike the idea of taking "creation" out of God's hands—an objection also commonly levelled against *in*

1. As of this writing, no further action has been taken on U.S. bills to ban all cloning.

*vitro* fertilisation or indeed abortion. Others feel that people will clone for selfish reasons, such as the desire to restore to life a dead child or parent or to have a handy tissue donor, rather than because of the simple desire for a child. Others again jib [balk] at the idea of creating a human being who is biologically a carbon copy of another.

For those who think that creating humans should be left entirely to the Almighty, the ethical case against cloning is cast-iron. For others, it is less clear-cut. There is currently a powerful case on safety grounds

*Scottish embryologist Ian Wilmut poses with the first cloned mammal, Dolly the sheep.*

*This Green party poster in Berlin depicts an army of cloned George Bushes and appeals to Germans with the message, "You decide! Don't give cloning a chance."*

for a moratorium on human experiments. But other arguments are weaker. A cloned child is likely to be a wanted child, offering hope to couples where one partner carries a deadly genetic mutation or existing fertility treatment is useless. To make a genetic copy of one parent or of one sibling is not very different from what nature already does with identical twins. And, although it may be wrong to create a child for selfish reasons, countless generations have seen their offspring as a workforce, pension plan or heir.

Once the evidence on animal cloning is more reassuring, governments should make human cloning subject to the same regulatory demands as any other experimental science. Human-cloning research could take place, tightly controlled, and progress like other experimental procedures, with strictly enforced licences for those who conduct research and harsh penalties for those who work without them. Embryos created in the course of human therapeutic cloning might also be studied to understand what happens, and what could go wrong, at the earliest stages of reproductive cloning.

## The Problem with Bans
To ban all cloning research, therapeutic as well as reproductive, as America proposes, is certainly a mistake. It scuppered [ruined] the UN's attempts to reach agreement on reproductive cloning alone. In any case, an indefinite ban on cloning research could have worse consequences than careful regulation. If Eve is indeed a copy of her mother, then the scientific hurdles to human cloning may be less formidable than is now

*In 2002 a group of paraplegics, who claim that their lives "hang in the balance," demonstrates before the Capitol, urging the Senate not to ban therapeutic cloning.*

believed. The goal of policy should be to ensure that research on cloning is conducted by those who know most about it, and about how to develop the technology, rather than by amateurs.

Like the war on drugs, bans on supply will not cut off demand. The desperation of infertile or bereaved couples is as all consuming as any craving for dope. The only hope of restraining this yearning will be to give such people hope, talking openly about the risks of cloning for mothers and babies, and explaining that the technology is advancing slowly but surely until it is safe. Only then may people wait, as they do for many experimental therapies, rather than turn to the renegades.

## EVALUATING THE AUTHORS' ARGUMENTS:

In the viewpoint you just read, the editors of the *Economist* compare a cloning ban to the war on drugs. Banning drugs, they contend, does not prevent people from wanting them. Why do you think the authors make this comparison? Is it a persuasive strategy?

# CHAPTER 2

# Should Therapeutic Cloning Be Pursued?

U.S. representative Dave Weldon calls for a ban on cloning in 2004.

# Therapeutic Cloning Is Ethical

**Gregory Stock**

*"[Therapeutic cloning] might save millions of real people suffering from real diseases."*

People can make sound ethical decisions about therapeutic cloning, claims Gregory Stock in the following viewpoint. In fact, he argues, because therapeutic cloning could relieve human suffering, prohibiting it demonstrates a greater disregard for human life. Many new developments such as organ transplants and test-tube babies seemed unnatural at first, but are now accepted, Stock maintains. Moreover, he asserts, people should not make decisions about therapeutic cloning based on a controversial religious debate about issues on which few people agree. Stock is director for the Program on Medicine, Technology, and Society at the University of California at Los Angeles School of Medicine.

**AS YOU READ, CONSIDER THE FOLLOWING QUESTIONS:**

1. In Stock's opinion, what could happen as a result of the theological debate about whether a tiny speck of cells is a human being?
2. What inconsistencies should congressional representatives see, in the author's view?
3. According to the author, where do the real dangers of biotechnology originate?

Gregory Stock, "Cloning Research Commentary," *LA Times,* December 2, 2001. Copyright © 2001 by Tribune Media Services, Inc. All rights reserved. Reprinted with permission.

[T]he November 26, 2001,] report of the first cloning of a human embryo had pundits wringing their hands. The announcement by a small biotech firm in Massachusetts, however, was pure hype. The researchers had not even formed viable human embryos—just fertilized eggs with their nuclei replaced that divided a few times, then died. Korean researchers reported the same thing [in 1998]. Such experiments are a long way from human cloning, since a few cellular divisions can occur even in the absence of viable chromosomes.

But the reports couldn't have come at a better time for Congress, which is eager to regulate this arena. . . . We have to hope that this time out they come up with something very different from the [David] Weldon bill, a draconian measure passed by the house [in July 2001, that failed in the Senate] that would have made scientists using cloning techniques in their quest for treatments for Parkinson's, diabetes, and other diseases subject to 10 years in prison. The bill also would have criminalized the importation of the products of such research, so if progress were made in Britain, where such research is legal, and Americans went there for treatment, they could be jailed upon their return for bringing home the cells in their flesh.

### The Role of Religion

It is frightening that an arcane theological debate about whether or not a tiny speck of cells is a human being could force a promising field of basic biomedical research to flee the United States for foreign countries. A consensus will never exist about moral questions of this sort.

> ## FAST FACT
>
> Some scientists hope that therapeutic cloning technology may some day be used to produce whole human organs from single cells or to raise animals having genetically altered organs suitable for transplanting to humans.

Even in the religious community, opinions differ. In Judaism and Islam, personhood begins about a month after conception, and before a proclamation by Pope Pius IX in 1869, even in Catholicism, ensoulment occurred not at conception, but after several weeks.

Religion has an important place in our hearts and lives, but it should not shape science policy. If Catholic dogma were our guide, birth control pills would be illegal; children of in-vitro fertilization would not exist, and evolution would only recently have been taught in school.

## Defying Common Sense

To oppose therapeutic cloning or its funding is one thing, to criminalize it quite another. It is beyond me how a majority of our

*The world's major religions differ in their beliefs as to when an embryo should be considered a human being.*

Views on embryonic stem cell research vary from one religion to the next. The following summarizes some of these views.

**Catholicism:** Because Roman Catholics view human life as a continuous progression from single-cell embryos to death, they object to extracting stem cells from aborted fetuses or spare embryos from fertility clinics, believing that human beings are being destroyed.

**Judaism:** Jewish law does not bestow legal status on embryos outside the womb. Fetuses are not recognized as human beings until they are born. Current stem cell research is thus permissible.

**Islam:** Islamic law does not define an embryo or specify when a fetus becomes a moral-legal being; thus if the purpose is to improve human health, stem cell research would be permissible.

**Protestantism:** Protestant faiths are split on stem cell research. Some believe that using stem cells from aborted fetuses or spare embryos exemplifies the strong using the weak, benefiting some over others. Other Protestant faiths claim that stem cell research should continue because of the benefit to humanity.

Congressional representatives could argue for this when it is legal for a woman to have an abortion or to discard an embryo for any reason whatsoever. Do they see no inconsistency in guarding the right to destroy a 3-month-old fetus, while putting a doctor in jail for an experiment on a microscopic dot of cells that could legally be flushed down a toilet?

To imbue a few cells in a Petri dish with human rights defies common sense. They lack a fundamental necessity for coming forth into our world—a connection to a warm, nurturing womb. Elevating their protection above the needs of medical research that might save millions of real people suffering from real diseases shows a profound disregard for human life.

Some argue that blocking this research will stop cloning. But they are deluding themselves. Over 300 animals have been cloned, some

# Stem Cells' Unlimited Potential

Researchers believe that human embryonic stem cells can be grown into a variety of body parts, enabling them to fight many common afflictions.

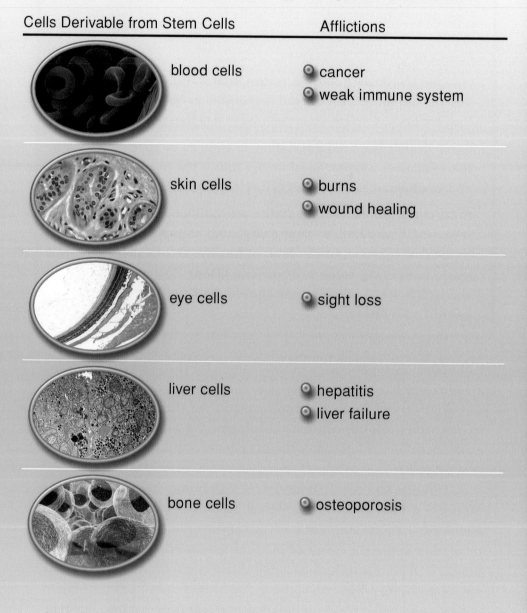

| Cells Derivable from Stem Cells | Afflictions |
| --- | --- |
| blood cells | cancer<br>weak immune system |
| skin cells | burns<br>wound healing |
| eye cells | sight loss |
| liver cells | hepatitis<br>liver failure |
| bone cells | osteoporosis |

Source: Adriel Bettelheim, *CQ Researcher,* December 17, 1999.

200 have survived, and most are healthy. Cloning a human is too dangerous at present, but wait a few years. We will see a human clone within the decade. And it won't destroy our values any more than a "test tube" baby did.

## Questioning Claims Against Cloning

Do people's brains go dead when they hear the word clone? I've seen otherwise sane individuals respond with diatribes about growing people to harvest their organs. But chopping an organ out of a clone would be just [as] much a murder as killing any other person. Clones are merely delayed identical twins. The idea is a bit strange, but clones are just not that threatening. You may already know one. Identical twins are clones, and though they're similar, they're unique individuals.

But perhaps clones are only the beginning. Might we not slide down a slippery slope into a dehumanized nightmare? Not as long as we remain capable of making nuanced moral judgments. And anyway, if this is a slippery slope, we are probably already on it. I suspect our path is more a slippery sidewalk. We may take a spill or two, but we'll get up, brush ourselves off, and continue on our way.

If human cloning is enough to bring down civilization, heaven help us, because throwing up obstacles to regenerative medicine is not going to save us. We are unraveling human biology, and many coming developments will be discomforting. But vaccines, antibiotics, organ transplants, and test-tube babies were each initially viewed as unnatural.

## Embracing the Future

We can't avoid the coming advances and wouldn't want to if we could. They offer too many potential benefits. The real question is not how we handle embryonic stem cells or genetically altered foods or any other specific technology, but whether we will continue to embrace the possibilities of the future or will pull back and relinquish these explorations to other braver souls in other regions of the world.

*The foal shown here with its adoptive mother was cloned with the genes of a champion Arabian stallion.*

We can choose to give up our leadership in medical research and watch the British or the Chinese set the course, but that will signal our decline. Our fall may take a while, but it will come.

In the aftermath of the World Trade Center [terrorist] attack [of September 11, 2001,] and the anthrax mailings [of November 2001], it is obvious that we face real enemies and dangers. Cloning and other advanced medical technologies, no matter how much they shake up our worldviews, are essentially on the side of life. They are intended to enhance our well being, not hurt us. The real dangers from biotech come not from this quarter, but from groups who have gone over to the dark side to weaponize ancient human enemies like plague and smallpox. We should not be so cavalier about stifling basic biomedical research, because ultimately, it may be what saves us.

## EVALUATING THE AUTHOR'S ARGUMENTS:

In the viewpoint you just read, Gregory Stock raises the possibility that biotechnological advances including cloning may be inevitable. What assurances does he make that these biotechnological advances will not be abused? Do you think these assurances are convincing? Explain.

# Therapeutic Cloning Is Unethical

### Linda K. Bevington

> *"We must not sacrifice one class of human beings (the embryonic) to benefit another (those suffering from serious illness)."*

Although some claim that therapeutic cloning will relieve human suffering, the practice is unethical because it requires the embryo's destruction, argues Linda K. Bevington in the following viewpoint. Moreover, she claims, therapeutic cloning's success is unproven while adult, nonembryonic, stem cells have shown great promise in treating diseases. Even if the stem cells of embryonic clones did relieve human suffering, sacrificing the life of some human beings to benefit others is unethical. Bevington, director of research for the Center for Bioethics and Human Dignity, contributed to the book *Genetics, Stem Cell Research, and Cloning: Are These Technologies Okay to Use?*

## AS YOU READ, CONSIDER THE FOLLOWING QUESTIONS:

1. In Bevington's view, what type of fetal stem cell research might be ethical?
2. According to the author, what obstacles have scientists conducting research on embryonic stem cells encountered?
3. What biblical passages does the author cite to explain why the human embryo should be valued?

Linda K. Bevington, "Stem Cell Research and 'Therapeutic' Cloning: A Christian Analysis," www.cbhd.org, September 2004. Copyright © 2002 by The Center for Bioethics and Human Dignity. Reproduced by permission.

In November of 1998, scientists reported that they had successfully isolated and cultured human embryonic stem cells—a feat which had eluded researchers for almost two decades. This announcement kicked off an intense and unrelenting debate between those who approve of embryonic stem cell research and those who are opposed to it. Some of the most prominent advocates of the research are scientists and patients who believe that embryonic stem cell research will lead to the development of treatments and cures for some of humanity's most pernicious afflictions (such as Alzheimer's disease, Parkinson's disease, heart disease, and diabetes). Among the most vocal opponents of the research are those who share the desire to heal, but who object to the pursuit of healing via unethical means. CBHD's [Center for Bioethics and Human Dignity's] view is that because human embryonic stem cell research necessitates the destruction of human embryos, such research is unethical—regardless of its alleged benefits. Ethical alternatives for achieving those benefits are available and should be actively pursued.

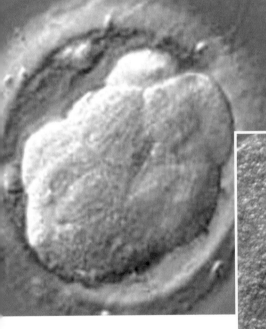

*Millions of stem cells (right) can be cultivated to form a single human embryo (above).*

### What Are Human Embryonic Stem Cells and How Are They Obtained?

Human embryonic stem cells are the cells from which all 200+ kinds of tissue in the human body originate. Typically, they are derived either from human embryos—usually those from fertility clinics who are left over from assisted reproduction attempts (e.g., in vitro fertilization). When stem cells are obtained from living human embryos, the harvesting of such cells necessitates destruction of the embryos.

### How Are Adult Stem Cells Different from Embryonic Stem Cells?

Adult stem cells (also referred to as "non-embryonic" stem cells) are present in adults, children, infants, placentas, umbilical cords, and cadavers. Obtaining stem cells from these sources does not result in certain harm to a human being.

### Is It Ethical to Obtain Stem Cells from Human Fetuses and Umbilical Cords?

Fetal stem cell research may ethically resemble either adult or embryonic stem cell research and must be evaluated accordingly. If fetal stem

*Protesters outside a 2002 cloning convention in San Diego condemn stem cell harvesters for playing God.*

cells are obtained from miscarried or stillborn fetuses, or if it is possible to remove them from fetuses still alive in the womb without harming the fetuses, then no harm is done to the donor and such fetal stem cell research is ethical. However, if the abortion of fetuses is the means by which fetal stem cells are obtained, then an unethical means (the killing of human beings) is involved. Since umbilical cords are detached from infants at birth, umbilical cord blood is an ethical source of stem cells.

### Have Scientists Been Successful in Using Non-Embryonic Stem Cells to Treat Disease?

Yes. In contrast to research on embryonic stem cells, non-embryonic stem cell research has already resulted in numerous instances of actual clinical benefit to patients. For example, patients suffering from a whole host of afflictions—including (but not limited to) Parkinson's disease, autoimmune diseases, stroke, anemia, cancer, immunodeficiency, corneal damage, blood and liver diseases, heart attack, and diabetes—have experienced improved function following administration of therapies derived from adult or umbilical cord blood stem cells. The long-held belief that non-embryonic stem cells are less able to differentiate into multiple cell types or be sustained in the laboratory over an extended period of time—rendering them less medically promising than embryonic stem cells—has been repeatedly challenged by experimental results that have suggested otherwise. . . .

### Have Scientists Been Successful in Using Embryonic Stem Cells to Treat Disease?

Though embryonic stem cells have been purported as holding great medical promise, reports of actual clinical success have been few. Instead, scientists conducting research on embryonic stem cells have encountered significant obstacles—including tumor formation, unstable gene expression, and an inability to stimulate the cells to form the desired type of tissue. It may indeed be telling that some biotechnology companies have chosen not to invest financially in embryonic stem cell research and some scientists have elected to focus their research exclusively on non-embryonic stem cell research.

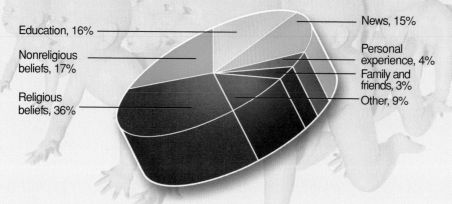

## Influences on Opinions About Cloning

According to polls, people form their opinions about cloning on the basis of many factors, although religious beliefs are the most prominent.

Education, 16%

Nonreligious beliefs, 17%

Religious beliefs, 36%

News, 15%

Personal experience, 4%

Family and friends, 3%

Other, 9%

Source: ABC News/Beliefnet Poll, August 2001.

### What Is the Relationship Between Embryonic Stem Cell Research and "Therapeutic" Cloning?

Another potential obstacle encountered by researchers engaging in embryonic stem cell research is the possibility that embryonic stem cells would not be immunologically compatible with patients and would therefore be "rejected," much like a non-compatible kidney would be rejected. A proposed solution to this problem is to create an embryonic clone of a patient and subsequently destroy the clone in order to harvest his or her stem cells. Cloning for this purpose has been termed "therapeutic" cloning—despite the fact that the subject of the research—the clone—is not healed but killed.

### Why Should We Value the Human Embryo?

Underlying the passages of Scripture that refer to the unborn (Job 31:15; Ps. 139:13–16; Isa. 49:1; Jer.1:5; Gal. 1:15; Eph. 1:3–4) is the assumption that they are human beings who are created, known, and uniquely valued by God. Genesis 9:6 warns us against killing our fellow human beings, who are created in the very image of God (Gen. 1:26–27). Furthermore, human embryonic life—as well as all of creation—exists primarily for God's own pleasure and purpose, not ours (Col. 1:16).

### Shouldn't It Be Ethical to Allow the Destruction of a Few Embryos in Order to Help the Millions of People Who Suffer from Diseases Such as Parkinson's and Heart Disease?

Many proponents of human embryonic stem cell research argue that it is actually wrong to protect the lives of a few unborn human beings if doing so will delay treatment for a much larger number of people who suffer from fatal or debilitating diseases. However, we are not free to pursue gain (financial, health-related, or otherwise) through immoral or unethical means such as the taking of innocent life (Deut. 27:25). The medical experiments in Nazi Germany should serve as just one reminder of the consequences of doing evil in the name of science. We must not sacrifice one class of human beings (the embryonic) to benefit another (those suffering from serious illness). Scripture resoundingly rejects the temptation to "do evil that good may result" (Rom. 3:8).

### What Does the Law Say?

No forms of stem cell research or cloning are prohibited by federal law, though some states have passed partial bans. Private funds can support any practice that is legal, whereas federal funds cannot be used for research on embryonic stem cell lines unless they existed before August 9, 2001.

## EVALUATING THE AUTHOR'S ARGUMENTS:

Linda K. Bevington cites biblical scripture to support her claim that embryonic cloning is unethical. The inset chart suggests religious beliefs figure prominently in people's opinions on cloning. What other factors in the inset chart are reflected in her viewpoint? Which factors do you find most persuasive?

VIEWPOINT

3

# Therapeutic Cloning Should Be Banned

**Wesley J. Smith**

*"Most Americans want to ban all human cloning."*

Research shows that therapeutic cloning is an inefficient process requiring hundreds of attempts to achieve success, claims Wesley J. Smith in the following viewpoint. Since millions of people suffer from diseases that therapeutic cloning might cure, the number of human embryos needed will be staggering, he maintains. Obtaining these embryos would require frightening methods such as obtaining eggs from the ovaries of aborted fetuses, which would promote abortion, Smith argues. To avoid such horrific possibilities, therapeutic cloning should be banned, he concludes. Smith, a fellow at the Discovery Institute, a pro-life, conservative think tank, is author of *The Culture of Death: The Assault on Medical Ethics in America.*

**AS YOU READ, CONSIDER THE FOLLOWING QUESTIONS:**

1. In Smith's view, why is therapeutic cloning doomed as a viable medical treatment?
2. According to the author, what is the risk of using animal eggs for therapeutic cloning?
3. What does the author think is a practical and moral alternative to therapeutic cloning?

Wesley J. Smith, "Therapeutic Dreaming: The False Promise of Experimental Cloning," *National Right to Life News,* vol. 30, October 2003. Copyright © 2003 by the National Right to Life Committee, Inc. Reproduced by permission of the author.

P olls show that most Americans want to ban all human cloning. President [George W.] Bush is eager to sign such a measure into law. The House has twice enacted a strong legal prohibition with wide, bipartisan votes. But cloning advocates have so far blocked passage of a ban in the Senate by asserting that "therapeutic cloning" might someday provide stem cell treatments for horrible illnesses such as Parkinson's and multiple sclerosis. (I believe the term "therapeutic cloning," is loaded and misleading. However, I use it here because the term is currently part of the popular lexicon.)

## How Therapeutic Cloning Would Work

According to the Biotechnology Industry Organization [BIO], the biotech industry's lobbying arm, here's how therapeutic cloning would work:

Suppose a middle-aged man suffers a serious heart attack while hiking in a remote part of a National Park. By the time he reaches the

*The reproductive cloning process can be extremely inefficient. In recent studies, more than one hundred attempts were made before a single embryonic stem cell line from a mouse was obtained.*

hospital, only a third of his heart is still working, and it is unlikely he will be able to return to his formerly active life. He provides scientists a small sample of skin cells. Technicians remove the genetic material from the cells and inject it into donated human eggs from which the chromosomes have been removed. These altered eggs [actually, cloned embryos] will yield stem cells that are able to form heart muscle cells. Since they are a perfect genetic match for the patient, these cells can be transplanted into his heart without causing his immune system to reject them. They grow and replace the cells lost during the heart attack, returning him to health and strength.

This scenario is typical of the hype that has pervaded discussions of therapeutic cloning over the last few years. But now, cold reality is setting in. Biotech researchers and cloning advocates are admitting difficulties in their professional journals, if not yet in the popular press, that make therapeutic cloning look more like a pipe dream than a realistic hope.

## An Inefficient Process

Consider a paper by Peter Mombaerts of Rockefeller University, "Therapeutic Cloning in the Mouse," . . . published by the National Academy of Sciences (NAS). Mombaerts has been investigating therapeutic cloning techniques in mice. It has been tough going. Of these efforts, he sadly reports, "The efficiency, or perhaps better, the lack of efficiency thereof, is remarkably consistent." It takes about 100 tries to obtain one viable cloned mouse embryonic stem cell line.

Mombaerts notes that creating human cloned embryos using "nuclear transfer is unlikely to be much more efficient" than it is in mice, especially given that "the efficiency of nuclear transfer has not increased over the years in any of the mammalian species cloned." Nuclear transfer, more precisely somatic cell nuclear transfer (SCNT), is the same procedure used to create Dolly the sheep. The nucleus from an egg is removed and replaced with the nucleus from a clone donor's somatic cell, such as a skin cell. The modified egg is stimulated with an electric current. If the cloning "works," a cloned embryo is created that then develops just like a naturally created embryo.

Given the significant difficulties researchers have already had, deriving cloned embryonic stem cell lines is likely to be far less efficient in humans than it has been in mice (assuming that it can be accomplished at all).

This is big news and let's hope senators are paying attention. If they are, it should sink the rival to [the] cynically misnamed Human Cloning Ban and Stem Cell Research Protection Act of 2003, which would not outlaw human cloning at all but would explicitly legalize it. If it takes 100 or more tries to make a single human cloned embryonic stem cell line, therapeutic cloning is all but doomed as a viable future medical treatment.

## Most People Do Not Support Human Cloning

**Question**: Should scientists be allowed to use cloning to create a supply of human embryos to be destroyed in medical research?

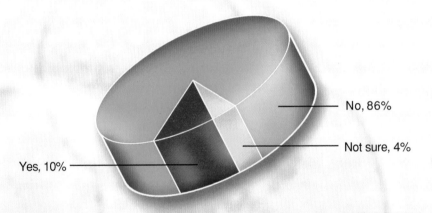

No, 86%

Not sure, 4%

Yes, 10%

**Question**: Do you think scientists should be allowed to clone human beings or not?

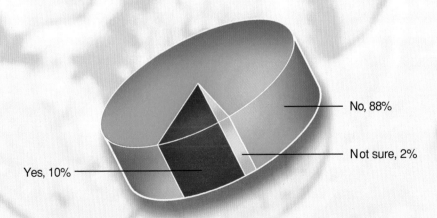

No, 88%

Not sure, 2%

Yes, 10%

Source: International Communications Research Poll, June 2001 (top); Time/CNN Poll, April 30, 2001 (bottom).

## Many Nations Support a Ban on All Human Cloning

On March 8, 2005, the United Nations General Assembly voted 84 to 34 in favor of a nonbinding statement calling for a total ban on human cloning, which would include therapeutic cloning. Some of the nations that voted in favor of the ban include Australia, Bolivia, Costa Rica, Ethiopia, Germany, Hungary, Iraq, Ireland, Italy, Mexico, Nicaragua, Philippines, Poland, Portugal, Rwanda, Saudi Arabia, Switzerland, Tajikistan, and the United States. Some of those that voted against the ban included Belgium, Brazil, Cambodia, Canada, China, Cuba, Democratic People's Republic of Korea, Denmark, Estonia, Finland, France, India, Jamaica, Japan, Netherlands, New Zealand, Norway, Republic of Korea, Singapore, Spain, Sweden, and the United Kingdom.

It's a simple matter of resources. There are more than 100 million Americans, according to the National Academy of Sciences, who might one day benefit from therapeutic cloning if all the high hopes for it panned out. Each therapeutic cloning attempt would require one human egg. If it takes 100 tries per patient for a cloned embryonic stem cell line to be successfully created, therapeutic cloning will never become a widely available therapy in medicine's armamentarium because there will never be enough eggs.

Do the math: 100 million patients at 100 eggs each would mean that biotechnologists would need access to at least 10 billion eggs just to treat the Americans the NAS has identified as having degenerative conditions that might respond positively to stem cell therapy. Even if we decided to strictly ration therapeutic cloning to, say, the sickest 100,000 patients, you would still need 10 million eggs! Even this strict rationing would require one million women of childbearing age to submit to egg extraction. These numbers are mind-boggling.

## The Potential Abuses of Cloning

Is there a way out of this egg dearth? Mombaert's article suggested two potentialities, to which I add a horrific third:

• Researchers could use animal eggs. Animal eggs are more readily available than human eggs, which would reduce the price of therapeutic cloning considerably. But using animal eggs would mean creating human embryos containing some nonhuman DNA. I doubt the American people would stand for this violation of nature's laws. (Mombaerts understates the case when he admits, "The idea of generating embryos with mixed human/animal properties, even transiently, is offensive to many people.") From a practical standpoint, the stem cells and indeed all tissues that would be extracted from such human/animal hybrids would contain nonhuman mitochondrial DNA. This could easily stimulate an auto-immune response or risk mitochondrial diseases in patients.

*An artist's rendition shows petri dishes containing perfectly identical embryos.*

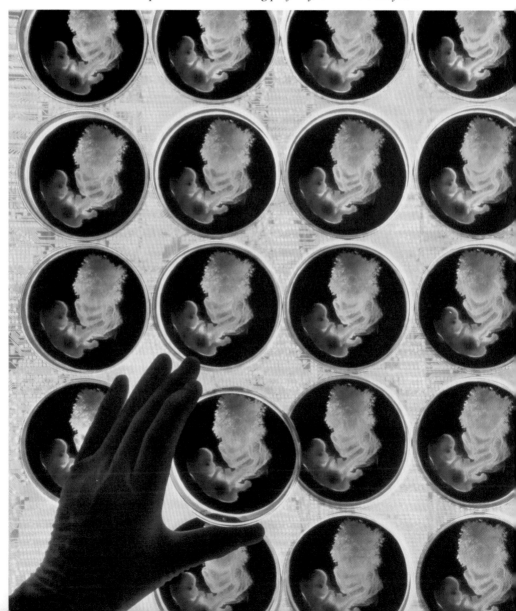

- Researchers might be able to learn how to transform embryonic stem cells taken from fertilized embryos into fully formed human eggs. This has been done in mice, but it will take many years to determine whether it can also be done with humans. But even if researchers learn how to morph stem cells into eggs, that does not mean they would be ready for use in cloning. Researchers would also have to ensure that they were not genetically defective and learn how to mature these eggs to the point where they would be usable for cloning. And even if they were able to learn how to do that, considering the huge number of eggs that would have to be produced in this way for therapeutic cloning to become widely available, morphing eggs out of embryonic stem cells hardly seems a plausible answer to the implacable egg dearth.

*A researcher in a California laboratory injects a chicken embryo with stem cells harvested from another chicken embryo.*

- Researchers could take the ovaries from female fetuses destroyed in late-term abortions, and maintain them in the hope of harvesting and maturing their eggs. I know this is revolting, but, sad to say, Dutch and Israeli researchers are already experimenting on this very thing with second- and third-trimester aborted fetuses, toward the goal of obtaining eggs for use in infertility treatments. Not only does this macabre research open the possibility that an aborted baby girl could become a mother, but if the procedure were perfected, it could result in aborted late-term female fetuses becoming a prime source of eggs for use in human cloning. As if that weren't troubling enough, the abortions of these female fetuses would have to be done in a way that did not damage their nascent ovaries, perhaps providing utilitarian impetus for the odious partial-birth abortion technique.

To pursue therapeutic cloning is to chase a mirage. On the other hand, adult stem cell research, a practical and moral alternative to therapeutic cloning, is already in human trials and moving ahead at tremendous speed. It was announced [in 2003], for example, that four out of five seriously ill human heart patients in a trial in Brazil no longer need heart transplants after being treated by their own bone marrow stem cells.

With all of the serious problems, both moral and practical, associated with human cloning, there is no longer any excuse for the current political impasse. The time has come for our senators to toss the phony cloning ban in the round file and pass the . . . [complete] ban [of all forms of human cloning] without further delay.

**EVALUATING THE AUTHOR'S ARGUMENTS:**

In the viewpoint you just read, Wesley J. Smith uses statistics to support his argument. Are these statistics persuasive? Explain why or why not.

# Therapeutic Cloning Should Not Be Banned

### Carl B. Feldbaum

*"Therapeutic cloning techniques are central to the production of breakthrough medicines, diagnostics and vaccines."*

Banning therapeutic cloning will hinder medical research, asserts Carl B. Feldbaum in the following viewpoint excerpted from testimony delivered before the U.S. Senate Commerce Committee. Few dispute that reproductive cloning should be banned, he argues, but other forms of cloning are very useful. Therapeutic cloning has the potential to produce cells that would repair or replace damaged cells, Feldbaum maintains. The U.S. Congress should therefore distinguish between reproductive and therapeutic cloning, he claims, so that scientists can pursue research that might relieve human suffering. Feldbaum is president of the Biotechnology Industry Organization (BIO), which represents companies and institutions devoted to biotechnology research and development.

**AS YOU READ, CONSIDER THE FOLLOWING QUESTIONS:**

1. According to Feldbaum, why would parental expectations be different for cloned children?
2. What are some of the diseases that disrupt cellular function or destroy tissue, in the author's opinion?
3. In the author's view, how does therapeutic cloning reduce the danger of testing the safety of new drugs?

Carl B. Feldbaum, testimony before the U.S. Senate Subcommittee on Science, Technology, and Space, Committee on Commerce, Washington, DC, May 2, 2002.

L et me begin by making my position perfectly clear: BIO opposes human reproductive cloning. It is simply too unsafe technically and raises far too many unresolved ethical and social questions.

## The Problem of Reproductive Cloning

That's why I wrote to President [George W.] Bush on February first [2001], urging him to extend the voluntary moratorium on human reproductive cloning, which was instituted in 1997. As I said in that letter, "Cloning humans challenges some of our most fundamental concepts about ourselves as social and spiritual beings. These concepts include what it means to be a parent, a brother, a sister and a family.

"While in our daily lives we may know identical twins, we have never experienced identical twins different in age or, indeed, different in generation. As parents, we watch with wonder and awe as our children develop

*Reporters snap photos as a team of Spanish researchers opens a container of embryonic stem cells shipped from an institute in Sweden.*

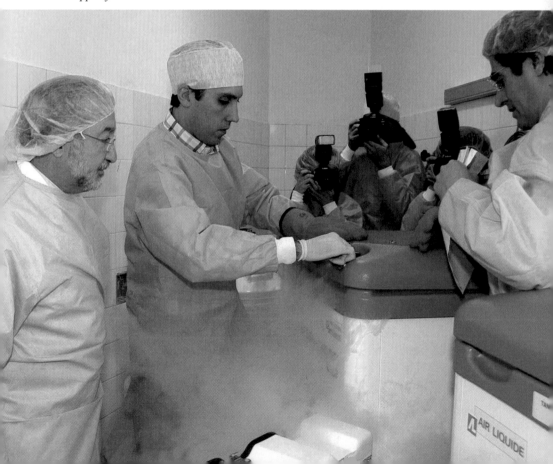

# FAST FACT

Scientists and commentators generally agree that reproductive cloning, or cloning with the intent to create live human births, should be off-limits. Attitudes toward therapeutic cloning are not that clear. According to an Ipsos-Reid poll published in December 2001, most Americans oppose unrestricted use of cloning but are split on whether to allow limited therapeutic cloning research. For example, 33 percent support a complete ban, 21 percent oppose any restrictions, and 39 percent believe research (therapeutic) cloning should be allowed.

into unique adults. Cloning humans could create different expectations. Children undoubtedly would be evaluated based on the life, health, character and accomplishments of the donor who provides the genetic materials to be duplicated. Indeed, these factors may be the very reasons for someone wanting to clone a human being." . . .

Perhaps even more compelling, it is extremely unsafe to attempt human reproductive cloning. In most animals, reproductive cloning currently has no better than a 3 to 5 percent success rate. In fact, scientists have been attempting to clone numerous species for the past 15 years with no success at all. What that means, simply and graphically, is that very few of the cloned animal embryos implanted in a surrogate mother animal survive. The others either die in utero —sometimes at very late stages of pregnancy—or die soon after birth. Only in cattle have we begun to achieve some improvement. What I am saying is that we cannot extrapolate to humans the data from the handful of species in which reproductive cloning is now possible. This grim record emphasizes just how unsafe this procedure is, whether it's applied to sheep, goats, dogs, cats, whatever.

I understand that it took over 270 attempts before Dolly [the first cloned mammal] was successfully cloned. Even if the odds of cloning a healthy child were brought down to one in three or one in two, it would be simply unacceptable. Rogue and grandstanding so-called scientists who claim they can—and will—clone humans for reproductive purposes insult the hundreds of thousands of responsible, reputable scientists who are working hard to find new therapies and cures for millions of individuals suffering from a wide range of genetic diseases and conditions.

The Food and Drug Administration (FDA) has publicly stated that it has jurisdiction over human reproductive cloning experiments and that it will not approve them. BIO supports that view and hopes that the next FDA commissioner—whoever that might be—will assert FDA's current statutory authority forcefully.

## The Beneficial Uses of Cloning Technology

Allow me to shift gears now, and make a critical distinction. It is critical to distinguish the use of cloning technology to create a baby—reproductive cloning—from therapeutic cloning. Therapeutic cloning techniques are central to the production of breakthrough medicines, diagnostics and vaccines to treat Alzheimer's, diabetes, Parkinson's, heart attacks, various cancers and hundreds of other genetic diseases. Therapeutic cloning could also produce replacement skin, cartilage and bone tissue for burn and accident victims and bring us ways to

*Researchers prepare unfertilized chicken eggs to receive injections of stem cells in the hopes that they can engineer a line of meatier chickens.*

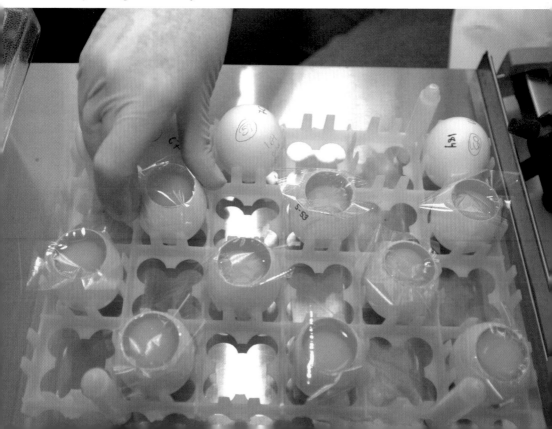

*Although therapeutic cloning could be used to produce life-saving medicines and generate new tissue, supporters claim that the technology is not capable of creating identical human beings.*

regenerate retinal and spinal cord tissue. Therapeutic cloning cannot produce a whole human being. This work should be allowed to move forward.

Allow me a minute or two to explain how therapeutic cloning can be used to develop products that will greatly improve the practice of medicine and, in turn, enormously improve the quality of life of individuals suffering from many of the most serious illnesses known to human kind.

Many diseases disrupt cellular function or destroy tissue. Heart attacks, strokes and diabetes are examples of common conditions in which critical cells are lost to disease. Today's medicine cannot completely restore this function. Regenerative medicine holds the potential to cause an individual's malfunctioning cells to work properly again or even to replace dead or irreparably damaged cells with fresh, healthy ones, thereby restoring organ function. The goal is to provide cells that won't be rejected when they are transplanted into the body.

Again, as I wrote in my letter to President Bush in February [2001], "To be perfectly clear, we support cloning of specific human cells, genes and other tissues that do not and cannot lead to a cloned human being." Therapeutic cloning technology can create pure populations of functional cells to replace damaged cells in the human body. Biomedical researchers are learning how to turn undifferentiated human stem cells into neurons, liver cells and heart muscle cells. Thus far, these human replacement cells appear to function normally in vitro, raising the possibility that they can be used in the treatment of devastating chronic diseases affecting these particular tissue types. This would, for instance, allow patients with heart disease to receive new heart muscle cells that would greatly improve cardiac function.

## The Potential of Cloning Techniques

Studies published in . . . *Science* magazine confirm the enormous potential of using cloning techniques in regenerative medicine. In those studies, which were done with mice, researchers were able to generate new neural cells and islets (insulin-producing cells). We hope to perfect these techniques to successfully transplant those cells. The potential benefit from this research to millions of people with diabetes, Parkinson's disease and spinal cord injuries is extraordinary.

Specific cellular cloning techniques, such as somatic cell nuclear transfer, are critical to these developments. They are necessary steps in producing sufficient quantities of vigorous replacement cells for the clinical treatment of patients, cells that could be transplanted without triggering an immune-response rejection.

Source: Keefe. © 2003 by Mike Keefe. All rights reserved. Reproduced by permission.

Companies also use therapeutic cloning techniques to develop research tools that help them determine if new drugs are safe for people. The use of normal, cloned human liver cells to test for certain toxic metabolites in drugs under development would reduce the danger of human clinical trials by eliminating such compounds before they are tested in humans. This process could both safeguard and streamline the drug development process, bringing drugs to patients sooner and more safely, and reduce the current reliance upon animal testing.

## Protecting Legitimate Research

. . . Congress has debated reproductive cloning before. After the unveiling of Dolly the sheep, a physicist named Richard Seed announced that he would perform human cloning experiments. The congressional debate that followed is instructive. At that time, a few senators introduced legislation that would have not only banned human reproductive cloning, but also would have prohibited critical meaningful, biomedical research. When opponents of the underlying bill staged a filibuster, supporters received only 42 votes for cloture. A review of the debate shows that while all senators opposed human reproductive cloning, a majority would not support far-reaching legislation that would—perhaps inadvertently—shut down important biomedical research.

As . . . Congress pursues legislative prohibitions on human reproductive cloning, we urge both caution and a distinction between reproductive and therapeutic cloning. We all agree that given the current safety and social factors, human reproductive cloning is repugnant. However, it is critical that in our enthusiasm to prevent reproductive cloning, we not ban vital research, turning wholly legitimate biomedical researchers into outlaws, and thus squelching the hope of relief for millions of suffering individuals.

Our nation is on the cusp of reaping the rewards from our significant investment in biomedical research. The U.S. biotech industry is the envy of much of the world, especially our ability to turn basic research at NIH [National Institutes of Health] and universities into applied research at biotech companies and in turn, into new therapies and cures for individual patients. Using somatic cell nuclear transfer and other cloning technologies, biotech researchers will continue to learn about cell differentiation, oocyte "reprogramming" and other areas of micro and molecular biology. Armed with this information, they can eventually crack the codes of diseases and conditions that have plagued us for hundreds of years, indeed, for millennia.

In conclusion, . . . human reproductive cloning remains unsafe, and the ethical issues it raises have not been reasonably resolved. The voluntary moratorium on human reproductive cloning should remain in place, and no federal funds should be used for human reproductive cloning. If the Congress in its wisdom decides that legislation to outlaw reproductive cloning is needed, that legislation must be carefully drawn to ensure that it will not stop vital research using therapeutic cloning.

**EVALUATING THE AUTHOR'S ARGUMENTS:**

In the viewpoint you just read, Carl B. Feldbaum says that he represents biotechnology companies, academic institutions, and state biotechnology centers. Does his affiliation with these institutions and organizations make his argument more or less persuasive? Explain.

# Embryonic Stem Cell Bans Discourage Life-Saving Research

**Simon Smith**

*"Stem cells from any embryos could soon provide treatments for diseases ranging from diabetes to Parkinson's."*

The U.S. government should not ban embryonic stem cell research because it may preserve human life, argues Simon Smith in the following viewpoint. Stem cell research, Smith claims, offers great promise for the treatment of diseases such as diabetes and Parkinson's. Moreover, research reveals that while the immune system rejects adult stem cells, it does not reject embryonic stem cells. A ban also takes control of stem cell research away from the government and gives private companies whose primary goal is to profit control over stem cell cures, he contends. Smith is the founder and editor-in-chief of Betterhumans, a company that provides information and opinion on advances in science and technology.

Simon Smith, "Time to End the Embryonic Stem Cell Ban," www.betterhumans.com, April 2, 2004. Copyright © 2004 by Simon Smith. Reproduced by permission.

AS YOU READ, CONSIDER THE FOLLOWING QUESTIONS:
  1. According to Smith, why did scientists attack the policy that limited research funding to only stem cell lines that already exist?
  2. What are many countries doing in response to the promise of embryonic stem cells, in the author's view?
  3. In the author's opinion, what kind of research environment has the stem cell ban created?

I t's been more than two years since US President George W. Bush addressed the nation to announce his embryonic stem cell policy. On August 9, 2001, from The Bush Ranch in Crawford, Texas, he teasingly began by noting the importance of federal funding. Then he revealed his hand, citing the "highest standards of ethics" in announcing strict federal funding limits. "Research on embryonic stem cells raises profound ethical questions, because extracting the stem cell destroys the embryo, and thus destroys its potential for life," he said.

## A Poor Compromise

The compromise: The government would fund research on 78 embryonic stem cell lines that already existed. There would be no money for new lines. "This allows us to explore the promise and potential of stem cell research without crossing a fundamental moral line, by providing taxpayer funding that would sanction or encourage further destruction of human embryos that have at least the potential for life," Bush said.

As we look back and around, it's strikingly apparent that this address is a milestone in the Bush administration's politicization and misuse of science, announcing one of its most regressive, deceptive and damaging policies. . . .

Almost immediately, scientists attacked the policy. Turns out that few of those promised stem cell lines were available, and probably none could be used for human trials. But the ban has stood, despite being a massive failure that smells of purposeful deception and has severely hurt not only promising medical research, but real people with real suffering. Meanwhile, private money is funding work on embryo research, private companies are getting wide-ranging patent rights, states are legislating to override the policy and, ban or no ban, embryos from fertility treatments are being destroyed anyway.

## A Potent Promise

While research on adult stem cells is progressing, embryonic stem cells are still far closer to use in regenerative treatments. Besides being less potent—a recent study stifled hope by finding that they can't replenish damaged heart muscle—adult stem cells are also harder to work with. Those from bone marrow or blood, for example, are highly variable, difficult to culture and rarely tolerated by a recipient's immune system when transplanted from a foreign donor.

*Bans on therapeutic cloning would jeopardize stem cell research at facilities such as this one in Kansas City, Missouri.*

Source: Britt. © by Copley News Service. Reproduced by permission.

Leaving aside stem cells from cloned embryos ("therapeutic cloning," as it's called, may prove financially prohibitive even if not legally prohibited, since it's so customized), stem cells from any embryos could soon provide treatments for diseases ranging from diabetes to Parkinson's. Human embryonic stem cells can be cultured indefinitely and appear to provoke no immune response in recipients—somehow, the immune system doesn't recognize them as foreign, as it does with adult stem cells.

In [one] study, for example, Richard Burt from Northwestern University in Chicago, Illinois and his colleagues reconstituted bone marrow and blood cells from embryonic stem cells even in genetically mismatched mice. If the finding, to be reported in *The Journal of Experimental Medicine*, holds true for humans, people wouldn't need genetically matched human bone marrow donors to fight leukemia, immune deficiencies and autoimmune diseases. A single line of embryonic stem cells could be cultured to provide treatments for many sufferers.

Recognizing such promise in embryonic stem cells, many countries are encouraging research with government oversight. In 1990, for example, the British Parliament created the Human Fertilisation and Embryology Authority to oversee embryo-related research and clinics, and later stem cell and cloning research. While few other countries have such organizations, many have taken a similar stance on the legality—and ethics—of embryonic stem cell research. China, Japan and Singapore even have regulations for embryonic stem cell research that allow therapeutic cloning while banning reproductive cloning. Canada's recently passed Bill C-6, which in its patchwork slapped-togetherness is by no means a model for anyone, at least allows the extraction of stem cells from excess embryos created for fertility treatments.

## FAST FACT

In May 2004 the world's first embryonic stem cell bank opened in Britain at the National Institute for Biological Standards and Control. The bank will store and grow cells and then distribute them to researchers around the world. Regulations on cloning and stem cell research vary across Europe and around the world. The most liberal rules apply in Britain, where scientists can apply for a license to clone human embryos in order to extract stem cells for medical research—therapeutic cloning.

## Stop the Insanity

The US could be a leader in stem cell research. This [2004] budget calls for the National Institutes of Health to receive about US$28 billion. Few countries, and no private companies, could match the kind of money that it could throw at *real* embryonic stem cell research—if it were allowed. And by funding the research, it could provide oversight and transparency.

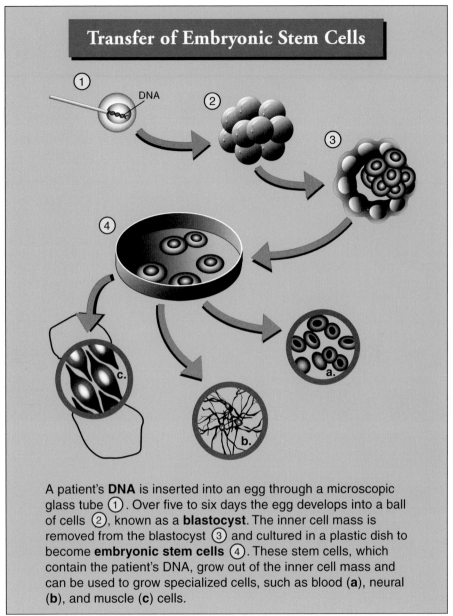

## Transfer of Embryonic Stem Cells

A patient's **DNA** is inserted into an egg through a microscopic glass tube ①. Over five to six days the egg develops into a ball of cells ②, known as a **blastocyst**. The inner cell mass is removed from the blastocyst ③ and cultured in a plastic dish to become **embryonic stem cells** ④. These stem cells, which contain the patient's DNA, grow out of the inner cell mass and can be used to grow specialized cells, such as blood (**a**), neural (**b**), and muscle (**c**) cells.

Source: University of Wisconsin-Madison/ The Why Files.

Instead, the stem cell ban has created an environment in which private companies can purchase tremendous intellectual property [rights over stem cell cures that might eventually lead to large profits] for little money while they pursue research in secrecy. In his excellent book *Merchants of Immortality,* Stephen Hall notes that the Bush ban paved the way for entrepreneurs to perform a "free-market override of the

*In 2004 voters in California approved $3 billion to fund stem cell research at research centers such as this one in La Jolla.*

congressional funding ban" that "completely transformed the technological landscape."

Hall notes, for example, that the ban gave Menlo Park, California-based *Geron* a huge amount of power over the future of stem cell research. "It positioned Geron to amass seemingly dominant commercial rights in the field," he says. Geron made an initial investment of as low as US$30,000, Hall says, that "would have potentially purchased a fabulously large patent estate [dominance over the profits received from stem-cell cures] for a relatively modest sum." This gave the company exclusive commercial rights to embryonic stem cell treatments for the heart, nervous system, liver, pancreas, blood-forming and bone-forming system. If a researcher used the company's cells to find a disease cure, it could claim the commercialization [profit making] rights and sue anyone who tried to bring the cure to market.

Make no mistake, the Bush ban hasn't stopped embryonic stem cell research. Besides private companies stepping in, several states, including California, have created or are considering creating legislation to keep various forms of embryonic stem cell research legal, including therapeutic cloning. And universities have begun setting up privately funded stem cell clinics.

All the ban has really done is slowed research, reduced government oversight, given private companies a nice gift, diminished information sharing and transparency and all but guaranteed that the US won't be a leader in stem cell treatments. And for no good reason, because excess embryos from fertility treatments are being destroyed anyway. Despite the Christian Right's attempts, there simply aren't enough people who want to adopt an embryo. Not only that, there are some couples who actually *want* their excess embryos used for research.

## EVALUATING THE AUTHOR'S ARGUMENTS:

In the viewpoint you just read, Simon Smith argues that a ban on embryonic stem cell research could turn the future of embryonic stem cell research over to private companies whose primary goal would be to maximize profits from stem cell cures by legally preventing other companies from competing—developing cures for a lower price. What evidence does Smith provide to support this claim? Do you think this evidence is convincing? Explain.

# The Benefits of Cloning Embryonic Stem Cells Are Exaggerated

**Harold Rex Greene**

*"Scientists have failed to demon-strate that they can remove cells from their rightful place in a human embryo and make them perform."*

The theory that scientists can program embryonic stem cells to cure diseases is simplistic and far-fetched, contends Harold Rex Greene in the following viewpoint. The genetic programming of cells is extremely complex, he argues, and the programmed stem cells that scientists plan to inject into humans will probably contain unknown genetic defects. The destruction of human embryos is therefore unwarranted, particularly when adult stem cell therapy, which does not sacrifice human embryos, has proven success, he claims. Greene, a clinical professor at the University of Southern California Keck School of Medicine, is consultant to the Council on Ethical Affairs of the California Medical Association.

Harold Rex Greene, "The Specious Logic of Embryonic Stem Cell Research," *National Right to Life News,* August 2004. Copyright © 2004 by the National Right to Life Committee, Inc. Reproduced by permission.

AS YOU READ, CONSIDER THE FOLLOWING QUESTIONS:
  1. According to Greene, what does the study of embryology demonstrate?
  2. Why does the author think that more and more embryonic stem "lines" will be needed for basic research?
  3. What problem would need to be solved in order to replace the nerves lost in ALS, in the author's view?

For over a decade, controversy has surrounded proposals to use human embryos to treat diseases such as Parkinson's and Alzheimer's. Scientists have publicly spoken about the "promise" of embryonic stem cells to cure diseases. That "promise" is based on the oft-repeated statement that human embryonic stem cells (often described as "master cells" or "blank cells") possess the unique ability to form all cell types in the human body. . . .

Many in the research community are enthusiastic supporters. While proponents pretend that the measure actually bans the use of funds for human cloning, in fact it merely constrains "human reproductive cloning" by not funding it. So-called "therapeutic cloning" would be made a constitutional right. It would not be banned, but would actually receive priority funding because it is not eligible for federal funds.

Both techniques produce cloned human embryos. With the latter, however, there is no intention to allow the birth of a human being.

## Faulty Science

This article will focus on the faulty science behind embryonic stem cell research which denies the astonishing complexity of embryonic development.

Many scientists have succumbed to a logical fallacy, based on a naive and simple-minded theory. From the obvious fact that embryonic cells eventually develop into all of the tissues in the body, they conclude that they can remove these cells and make them rebuild damaged, diseased organs in other people's bodies. To describe this exercise in science fiction they have hijacked the term "regenerative medicine."

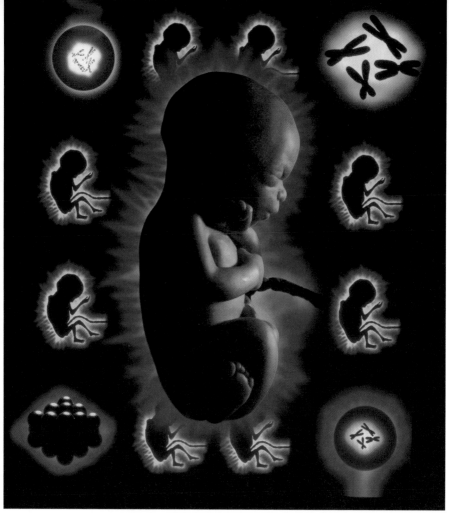

*Cloning opponents claim that the messaging system that tells stem cells where to go and what to do is too complex to be duplicated safely.*

But their belief is utterly without what scientists call proof of concept, that is, animal studies that confirm their theory. On the contrary, animal studies have gone on for nearly 20 years and proved quite disappointing.

## A Complex System

To understand why requires a brief overview of the incredibly complicated messaging system that makes embryonic cells usually go where they need to go and do what they're supposed to do.

During the first eight weeks the embryo changes from a single-celled zygote to a fully formed fetus. The study of embryology demonstrates an amazing choreography, like a symphony with millions of musicians in constant motion, adding more and more players, who change instruments yet never miss a beat.

A variety of signals direct cells to grow, migrate, differentiate, and spontaneously die. Some cells serve only as temporary placeholders while others take up permanent residence at their target organ. Some of the messages that determine embryonic development are intrinsic—locked in the genetic code. Some are extrinsic—physical, chemical, and electrical messages between adjacent cells jostling for position.

Much of our genetic code is dedicated to embryonic development and shuts down once a fetus has formed. The reactivation of these genes in the wrong time and place can be disastrous. Mutations in a single cell, allowing such reactivation, can result in malignancies.

*This young boy was treated for sickle-cell anemia, an exceedingly painful genetic blood disease, using stem cells harvested from the umbilical cord of a healthy baby.*

Cloning illustrates this complexity. In cloning, the nucleus of a human ovum (egg) is removed and replaced with the nucleus from a body cell. The theory is that the surrounding cytoplasm will "reprogram" the replacement nucleus to revert to its former embryonic functions.

However, most of the time this fails because the transferred nucleus has already been programmed to serve its adult function. This role is by no means simple. For example, as a cheek cell it must constantly replace the lining of the mouth, maintaining a perfect balance of cell growth and death.

It is nothing short of hubris to believe that we can rip embryonic cells out of their normal context in the embryo, inject them into a "host" body, and expect them to perform perfectly every time.

## The Risks

On occasion, a cloned animal embryo develops that can be implanted in a uterus and grown to term. Sometimes bizarre monsters develop that kill the host mother. But a few cloned animals do make it to term—

*It took 277 attempts to clone Dolly the sheep, who was euthanized after it was discovered that she had a progressive lung disease.*

most, if not all, carrying severe defects. If that same cloned embryo is destroyed for stem cells instead, those stem cells will carry severe defects—defects that arise from short-circuiting normal development and activating a human being's genetic code all at once.

Cells obtained from blastocysts (one-week-old embryos) created in IVF [in vitro fertilization] fare little better. The tissue cultures into which these cells are placed lack the features of the embryonic environment which had orchestrated the development of the cells. Wrenched out of this setting, the cells spontaneously differentiate into precursors of adult tissues: kidneys, hearts, nerves, or, worst of all, tumors. No one would dare inject them into a person. Hence, more and more embryonic stem "lines" will be needed just for basic research.

## FAST FACT

It takes more than 100 eggs to produce a useable stem cell line at therapeutic cloning's present stage of development. Thus, if a cure for diabetes involving embryonic stem cells is found, it would take 1.5 billion eggs to cure the 15 million Americans who have diabetes.

In short, scientists have failed to demonstrate that they can remove cells from their rightful place in a human embryo and make them perform according to their wishes. There is strong evidence suggesting that we will never be able to do this.

The fallacy of embryonic stem cell research collapses on closer examination. For example, in a patient with Lou Gehrig's disease (amyotrophic lateral sclerosis or ALS), an immune reaction destroys the nerves in the brain and spinal cord that control muscles. Such a patient could receive embryonic nerve cells that would supposedly replace the dead nerves.

To create genetically matched stem cells, proponents propose to create cloned embryos, which, in theory, would not be rejected. But there are numerous problems.

As recent experiments in South Korea demonstrate, to create cloned embryos, dozens of eggs (if not hundreds more) will be needed, no doubt purchased from women who've undergone super-ovulation. From those eggs a few embryos will successfully develop via nuclear transfer (cloning), which means that identical twins will be created for the purpose of salvaging body parts.

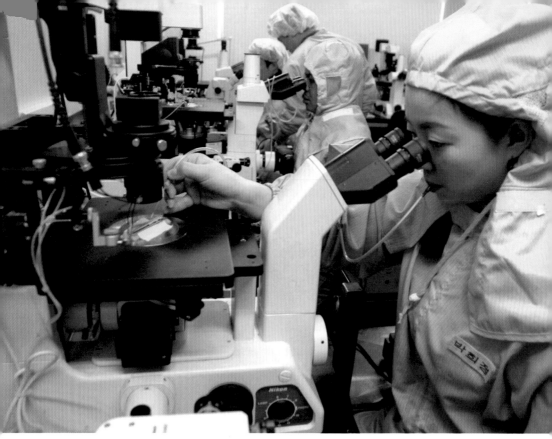

*Researchers at Seoul National University work to clone human embryos in order to harvest stem cells.*

The patient then receives many cloned embryonic cells, virtually all of which most likely have significant genetic defects. Remember, if a single cell misfires, the result of the experiment could be an artificial cancer. Moreover, if the cells miraculously fail to degenerate into cancer cells, other problems remain.

Lou Gehrig's disease has a rapid course, but it takes nerves years to grow back. Meanwhile the disease is still attacking the nervous system and the injected cells. In other words, before this approach could hope to replace the nerves lost in ALS, we would first have to correct the problem that makes the body attack its own nerve cells in the first place.

Why engage in this Faustian bargain of destroying human life for the benefit of others? The truth is that biotech entrepreneurs and ambitious scientists hope to profit from mass-produced cellular therapies at taxpayers' expense. To bolster their feeble theory they make vastly exaggerated claims and cite heart-rending testimonials in lieu of scientific proof.

## The Promise of Adult Stem Cells

Sadly, all this is unnecessary. Adult stem cells (including cord blood) already are a 30-year success story. They've gone through natural embryonic development in the patient's own body, and have preserved the ability to self-renew and proliferate as needed.

Recent experiments have even shown that transplanted adult bone marrow stem cells integrate quite nicely into other organs and tissues (heart and brain, for example). They are simply "switching jobs."

The embryonic stem cell entrepreneurs know their venture is extremely speculative. What they don't realize is that they are actually building the equivalent of a 21st century *Titanic*.

The fact remains that embryonic cells are likely to perform their natural role only in the context of the intact, developing embryo, not as so many harvested crops. Our public resources should be directed towards the development of therapies that have a chance to succeed and carry no moral baggage—adult and cord-blood stem cells.

## EVALUATING THE AUTHORS' ARGUMENTS:

In the viewpoint you just read, Harold Rex Greene argues that the messaging system that directs embryonic cell development is too complicated for scientists to engineer. What evidence does he provide to support this claim? Is the evidence that Greene provides as proof that embryonic stem cell research will fail to provide promised cures more convincing than Simon Smith's evidence in the previous viewpoint that embryonic stem cell research will succeed? Explain.

# CHAPTER 3

# Should Animal Cloning Be Pursued?

*A number of animals, including pigs, cattle, cats, goats, horses, and sheep, have been successfully cloned.*

**VIEWPOINT**

**1**

# Pet Cloning Can Be Ethical

### Lou Hawthorne

*"Our primary ethical concerns are . . . pragmatic: Are we increasing or decreasing the suffering of animals?"*

Pet cloning can be done ethically, argues Lou Hawthorne in the following viewpoint. In response to the demand for pet cloning, Hawthorne and others created Genetic Savings & Clone (GSC), a California company that clones pets and livestock. According to Hawthorne, the company's code of ethics ensures that surrogate mothers are treated well and later adopted. Hawthorne adds that by buying the eggs of spayed animals, GSC does its part to help pet overpopulation. The company's main concern is how to deal with the risk of genetic abnormalities, and GSC, Hawthorne contends, invests millions to assess these problems in the embryo's early stages.

**AS YOU READ, CONSIDER THE FOLLOWING QUESTIONS:**

1. According to Hawthorne, on what did the Missyplicity team agree during its initial ethical discussions?
2. How is GSC's code of ethics different for pets and livestock animals, in the author's opinion?
3. In the author's view, what leading theory is used to explain genetic abnormalities in clones?

Lou Hawthorne, "A Project to Clone Companion Animals," *Journal of Applied Animal Welfare Science,* vol. 5, 2002. Copyright © 2002 by Genetic Savings & Clone. All rights reserved. Reproduced by permission.

Genetic Savings and Clone [GSC] has its roots in the Missyplicity Project, a $3.7 million scientific research project aimed at cloning a specific mixed breed dog named Missy, owned by an anonymous—though obviously very wealthy—individual. As Project Coordinator of Missyplicity, my first task was to recruit a world-class scientific team, a process that began in August of 1997 and culminated several months later with the selection of a team based at Texas A&M University, which has a strong animal science program.

The Missyplicity sponsor, though an educated man, is not an ethicist; the sum of our initial ethical discussions was an agreement that it would not be right for other dogs to suffer simply to replicate his aging spayed mutt. Knowing that, historically, academic animal researchers haven't exactly been a dog's best friend, I decided that we would need a Code of Bioethics to safeguard the welfare of animals associated with the Missyplicity Project. This code would have to be a binding exhibit to our funding agreements, which was, and still is, the case.

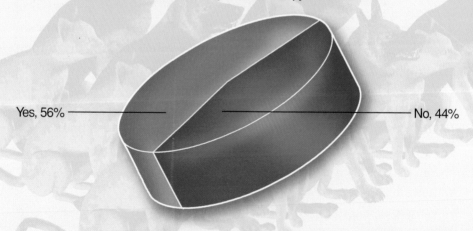

## Pet Owners Divide on Cloning Pets

**Question:** If a company announced that a perfect copy of your pet could be made when the pet got old or died, would you order a copy or not?

Yes, 56% —————— —————— No, 44%

Source: Fox News/Opinion Dynamics, February 19, 2002.

## Time Line of Cloning Technology

Cloning technology has been over one hundred years in the making.

**1894** Hans Dreisch isolated the cells of two- and four-cell sea urchin embryos and observed them develop into small but complete larvae.

**1901** Hans Spemann split a two-cell newt embryo into two parts, successfully producing two larvae.

**1952** Robert Briggs and Thomas J. King transplanted the nucleus of a frog embryo cell into an unfertilized egg cell with the nucleus removed. These injected eggs developed into tadpoles and many grew into juvenile frogs. This technique, nuclear transfer, became the prototype for cloning of multicelled organisms.

**1986** Steen Willadsen cloned lambs by fusing the nucleus of an eight-cell embryo to an egg cell with the nucleus removed. Other researchers subsequently succeeded in producing full-term cattle, sheep, pigs, goats, and rats using a similar approach.

**1997** Ian Wilmut and his colleagues from Scotland produced Dolly, the first mammal cloned from an adult cell.

**2001** The world's first cloned companion animal, a cat named "CC," was born in Texas. The project was funded by Genetic Savings & Clone.

## Facing a Paradox

Not long after the research began, the British Broadcasting Company did a story about Missyplicity—the first of many to come. At the time, we discovered the paradox that forms the core of GSC's business model: Millions of people believe they have a one-in-a-million pet. Swamped with thousands of phone calls and emails, we quickly realized that we were dealing with something much bigger than cloning a single pet: the commodification of cloning, with profound ethical, social, and, of course, commercial implications.

On February 16, 2000, we launched GSC. The stated mission was the development/refinement of cloning technology for what we termed the Big Four: cats and dogs in our Pet Division and horses and cattle in our Livestock Division. We also made a public commitment to transfer this species-specific cloning knowledge to organizations working to repopulate endangered relatives of the Big Four and to groups

*Lou Hawthorne, CEO of Genetic Savings & Clone, the first company to offer commercial pet cloning services, poses in front of a picture of Carbon Copy, the first cloned domestic cat.*

engaged in breeding of exceptional assistance dogs—whether for people with disabilities or for search and rescue work.

## Creating a Code of Ethics

We also gave GSC a Code of Ethics—actually two codes reflecting the highly divergent value systems our culture embraces for pets on one hand and livestock on the other. For example, GSC's Pet Code of Ethics, like the Missyplicity Code, requires playtime and enrichment for surrogates while under our care, followed by adoption into a loving home after a reasonable service period. Such guidelines simply make no sense within an agricultural setting. Thus, we decided that the GSC Codes for each division would reflect the highest values within the relative contexts of pet and livestock breeding. For instance, though we at GSC do not adopt out our bovine surrogates, we do guarantee that their quality of life is measured against the standards of traditional farming versus the far lower standards of modern factory farming.

Although we are often asked abstract ethical questions such as "Aren't you playing God?" and "Isn't this cheating Death?" it should be clear that our primary ethical concerns are more pragmatic: Are we increasing or decreasing the suffering of animals? Maintaining the physical and psychological well-being of our surrogates is only part of our challenge: We must consider both the implications of replicating pets when so many are homeless, and the risk of creating nonhuman animals with genetic abnormalities.

## The Problem of Pet Overpopulation

Cloning companion animals has far more symbolic than actual significance in terms of pet overpopulation. It will likely be decades—if ever—before pet cloning is inexpensive enough to affect the population of unwanted pets to any measurable degree. Regardless, GSC has made a public commitment to "reduce the population of unwanted pets to a greater degree than our cloning activities add to the problem." The cloning process itself obviates this commitment: For every individual animal we clone, we need thousands of eggs of that species for the cloning process. For pet species, we purchase these eggs from spay clinics—hundreds of thousands of dollars worth each year for research alone. These funds underwrite the spaying of far more dogs and cats than we could ever hope to create by cloning.

The ethical issue of greatest concern in moving forward is the risk of creating animals with genetic abnormalities. Roughly 20% of cattle clones which survive long enough to be detectable in utero go on to exhibit some sort of health problem. Some miscarry, others die

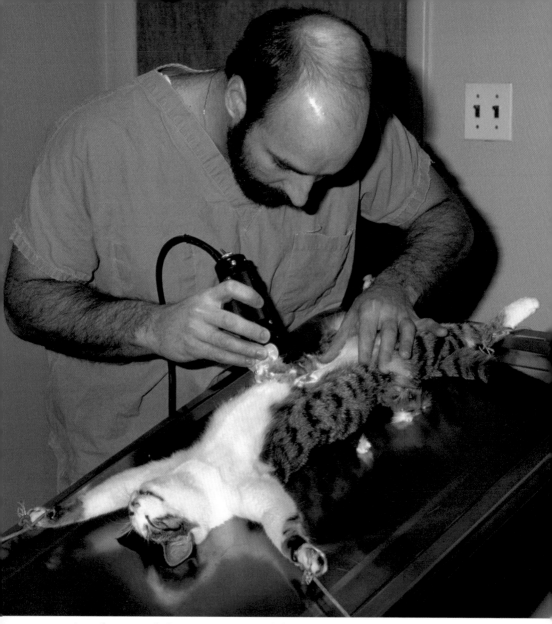

*A vet shaves a cat before spaying it. Animal cloners obtain the eggs needed to clone companion animals from spay clinics.*

shortly after birth, others develop later stage health problems, whereas still others outgrow neonatal problems and develop normally. A leading theory holds that the vast majority of these problems trace back to some sort of genetic "misexpression"—that is, incomplete or inaccurate reprogramming of the donor cell by the egg resulting in certain embryonic genes being "on" when they should be "off" or vice versa.

## Considering the Risks

There are three factors to consider with regard to genetic abnormalities in clones:

- Considerable evidence shows that such problems may be species-specific; Louisiana State University has cloned numerous goats yet has seen none of the abnormalities commonly observed in cattle clones. At this time, we do not know whether cloned pet species will exhibit such health problems.

- Different cloning techniques seem to yield better results than others, which is why we are building sophisticated software for tracking and analyzing the hundreds of variables involved in the cloning process.

- Genetic abnormalities may be detectable in the early embryo stage prior to transfer into a surrogate; thus, we are investing millions of dollars into new technologies for assessing gene expression and other key parameters of embryo viability.

Our ethical bottom line is this: Cloning, like many activities, can have either positive or negative impact based on the level of awareness we bring to the process and the amount of responsibility we take for the consequences of our actions.

## EVALUATING THE AUTHOR'S ARGUMENTS:

In the last paragraph of the text you just read, Lou Hawthorne maintains that whether the cloning activities of GSC have a positive or negative impact is based on the amount of responsibility the company takes for the consequences of its actions. Do the arguments in favor of pet cloning that he makes in the text convince you that GSC takes responsibility for the consequences of its actions? Explain why or why not.

# Pet Cloning Is Unethical

## Randy Burkholder

*"Pet cloning . . . is a small and selfish wrong [that] certainly will lead to greater evils."*

Pet cloning teaches children that satisfying their desires is more important than learning to deal with the losses they will experience in life, claims Randy Burkholder in the following viewpoint. Despite claims by pet cloning companies that cloning is an alternative form of reproduction, the actual objective of pet owners is to resurrect their pets, Burkholder maintains. Moreover, he argues, if creating baby pets is the real goal, than cloning humans for the same reason may be the next logical step. Burkholder is a medical and science writer.

**AS YOU READ, CONSIDER THE FOLLOWING QUESTIONS:**
1. In Burkholder's opinion, what on the Lazaron Bio Technology Web site suggests that pet owners want to resurrect, not reproduce their pets?
2. According to the author, to what are children growing blind?
3. In the author's view, what do cloning advocates think will happen to people once they become comfortable with pet cloning?

Randy Burkholder, "Painful Lessons of Pet Cloning," *Washington Times,* April 15, 2002. Copyright © 2002 by the *Washington Times.* All rights reserved. Reproduced by permission of Valeo IP.

"The dog of your boyhood," Mississippi author Willie Morris said, "teaches you a great deal about friendship, and love and death."

My pure-bred beagle, which in a moment of unparalleled inspiration I named "Beagle," died chasing an orange VW Bug when I was 9. His sudden passing taught me lessons I still carry with me today.

## Cloning Cats

But never mind all that. Soon we can spare our children this calamity—and deny them the lessons that come with it. The clever scientists at Texas A&M University have succeeded for the first time in human history (and I don't use the term lightly) in cloning a cat, and given it the cute name "Cc," for Carbon copy. (One can't help but

*Two vets from Texas A&M University pose with Carbon Copy, the first product of a program designed to allow pet owners to clone their beloved companions.*

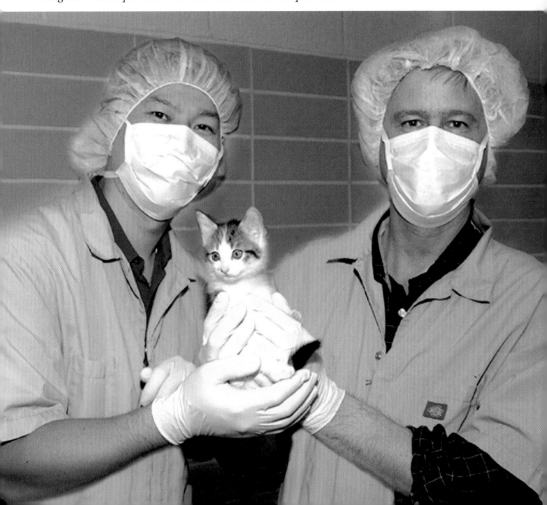

wonder if the name isn't descriptive of the researchers' view of all life forms—mere arrangements of carbon-based molecules awaiting scientific "enhancement".)

And close behind come the clever scientist-entrepreneurs forming cute corporations like Genetic Savings and Clone and PerPETuate, promising to spin DNA strands into bottom-line gold. Genetic Savings and Clone, in fact, says it expects "to begin commercial cat cloning on a very limited case-by-case basis later [in 2002]."

The Texas A&M researchers were quick to point out that Cc is not an exact replica of the cat that was the source of the original egg cell. We used to say "mother." I guess "source of the original egg cell" is more descriptive now. "This is reproduction, not resurrection," one of the researchers said.

## Resurrection or Reproduction?

But companies need investors, and reporters need stories, so this subtlety is soon glossed over. Reporting on the news of Cc, ABC News said, "Keeping a beloved pet part of the family for decades may become a reality."

Source: Sack. © 2004 by the *Star Tribune*. Reproduced by permission.

The very name of one cloning start-up, Lazaron Bio Technologies—a not-so-subtle allusion to the Biblical story of Lazarus—suggests that resurrection, at least on an emotional level, is indeed the goal. Lazaron's web site, in fact, offers "Saving Your Animal's Life" as its first menu selection. Elsewhere on the site the firm asks, "Does you loved animal's genetic character have to die? No, it can live on." Tabby, come forth.

You can put any qualms you may have to rest, however, because Genetic Savings and Clone, at least, is "committed to performing this work to the highest ethical standards." This no-doubt heartfelt commitment is, well, less than reassuring.

Ultimately it doesn't matter whether the clone is a perfect resurrection or just a genetic match, or whether the work is performed according to "the highest ethical standards." Genetic misconceptions and spurious bioethics codes skirt the basic issue, which is not how pet cloning is understood, or how it is performed, but whether it should be performed at all. I commend Genetic Savings and Clone for its commitment to excellence in its work, I just think it should find a different line of business.

**FAST FACT**

It takes a great many embryos to clone an animal. Below is a list of animals and the number of embryos needed to produce one clone.

| Sheep | 277 |
| Mouse | 942 |
| Cattle | 10 |
| Goat | 112 |
| Rhesus Monkey | 107 |
| Pig | 110 |
| Cat | 87 |
| Rabbit | 1,084 |

## Lessons Lost

If a pet's death is quickly followed by a cloned copy, the lessons children learn will be very different from those I was taught by Beagle.

When Beagle died, I learned that death is final, that in life there is pain that we can either flee or overcome. I first began to understand that the legacy of our days in this world is ultimately irrevocable, and so life is supremely precious.

The unspoken lessons we will teach our children through pet cloning are that even life itself should be bent to their desires; that the avoidance of pain is the ultimate good; that death is revocable, and life therefore disposable.

*In 2004 a Texas woman paid $50,000 for Little Nicky, the clone of her diseased cat, Nicky.*

Genetic "enhancement" of pets (think hot-pink kitties and glow-in-the-dark bunnies) presents the same problem. Already our children grow blind to the spectacular diversity of the beauty that is all around them in nature, and see beauty only in their own desires.

Pet cloning is certainly not the biggest problem we as a society face. It is a small and selfish wrong. But it certainly will lead to greater evils.

Advocates of the practice suggest that cloning pets is a way to make people more comfortable with the technology and ultimately with human cloning. Professor Lee Silver, that paragon of bioethical restraint from Princeton University, said in a BBC News story, "The incredible thing is that if you can perfect the technology in lots of different animals it makes it that much more likely it's going to move to human beings."

Genetic Savings and Clone helpfully closes the circle from the other direction, pointing out that "cloning is simply the latest form of assisted reproduction, not all that different from artificial insemination and in vitro fertilization—which were also controversial when first introduced." We're cloning cats. We're creating babies through in vitro fertilization. Why not take the next logical step and clone humans?

How we welcome life into this world and mark its passing are measures of our human dignity, and cloning touches on them both. Pet cloning offers a gentle first step beneath this dignity.

## EVALUATING THE AUTHOR'S ARGUMENTS:

Near the end of the essay you just read, the author asks, "Why not take the next logical step and clone humans?" Does this strategy make his argument more or less persuasive? Explain.

# Cloning Could Save Endangered Species

## Robert P. Lanza, Betsy L. Dresser, and Philip Damiani

*"Cloning endangered species . . . has an important place in plans to manage species that are in danger of extinction."*

Robert P. Lanza, Betsy L. Dresser, and Philip Damiani claim in the following viewpoint that cloning provides a new way to preserve endangered species. Although preserving the habitat of endangered species is important, some countries are too poor or unstable to do so, thus storing the genetic stock of threatened animals from these countries may be the only way to preserve at risk species, the authors argue. Lanza is vice president of Advanced Cell Technology (ACT); Dresser is director of the Audubon Institute Center for Research of Endangered Species; Damiani, a research scientist at ACT, is a member of the International Embryo Transfer Society.

**AS YOU READ, CONSIDER THE FOLLOWING QUESTIONS:**
1. According to the authors, why must researchers get cells from two different species to yield the clone of one?
2. Why is cloning not as easy in practice, in the authors' view?
3. In the authors' opinion, what species will be the first to be cloned?

Robert P. Lanza, Betsy L. Dresser, and Philip Damiani, "Cloning Noah's Ark," *Scientific American,* November 29, 2000. Copyright © 2000 by Scientific American, Inc., www.sciam.com. All rights reserved. Reproduced by permission.

In late November [2000] a humble Iowa cow is slated to give birth to the world's first cloned endangered species, a baby bull to be named Noah. Noah is a gaur: a member of a species of large oxlike animals that are now rare in their homelands of India, Indochina and southeast Asia. These one-ton bovines have been hunted for sport for generations. More recently the gaur's habitats of forests, bamboo jungles and grasslands have dwindled to the point that only roughly 36,000 are thought to remain in the wild. The World Conservation Union–IUCN Red Data Book lists the gaur as endangered, and trade in live gaur or gaur products—whether horns, hides or hooves—is banned by the Convention on International Trade in Endangered Species (CITES).

But if all goes as predicted, . . . a spindly-legged little Noah will trot in a new day in the conservation of his kind as well as in the

*Cloning proponent Dr. Robert P. Lanza argues that cloning can help preserve endangered species.*

*Animal cloning researchers hope to use the technology to bring endangered species, such as the panda, back from the brink of extinction.*

preservation of many other endangered species.[1] Perhaps most important, he will be living, mooing proof that one animal can carry and give birth to the exact genetic duplicate, or clone, of an animal of a different species. And Noah will be just the first creature up the ramp of the ark of endangered species that we and other scientists are currently attempting to clone: plans are under way to

1. Noah was born on January 8, 2001. Noah died 48 hours later of dysentery, which scientists claim was unrelated to the cloning.

clone the African bongo antelope, the Sumatran tiger and that favorite of zoo lovers, the reluctant-to-reproduce giant panda. . . .

## Protecting Genetic Diversity

Advances in cloning offer a way to preserve and propagate endangered species that reproduce poorly in zoos until their habitats can be restored and they can be reintroduced to the wild. Cloning's main power, however, is that it allows researchers to introduce new genes back into the gene pool of a species that has few remaining animals. Most zoos are not equipped to collect and cryopreserve [preserve by freezing] semen; similarly, eggs are difficult to obtain and are damaged by freezing. But by cloning animals whose body cells have been preserved, scientists can keep the genes of that individual alive, maintaining (and in some instances increasing) the overall genetic diversity of endangered populations of that species.

Nevertheless, some conservation biologists have been slow to recognize the benefits of basic assisted reproduction strategies, such as in vitro fertilization, and have been hesitant to consider cloning. Although we agree that every effort should be made to preserve wild spaces for the incredible diversity of life that inhabits this planet, in some cases either the battle has already been lost or its outcome looks dire. Cloning technology is not a panacea, but it offers the opportunity to save some of the species that contribute to that diversity. A clone still requires a mother, however, and very few conservationists would advocate rounding up wild female endangered animals for that purpose or subjecting a precious zoo resident of the same species to the rigors of assisted reproduction and surrogate motherhood. That means that to clone an endangered species, researchers such as ourselves must solve the problem of how to get cells from two different species to yield the clone of one.

## A Not So Simple Process

It is a deceptively simple-looking process. A needle jabs through the protective layer, or zona pellucida, surrounding an egg that hours ago resided in a living ovary. In one deft movement, a research assistant uses it to suck out the egg's nucleus—which contains the majority of a cell's genetic material—leaving behind only a sac of gel called cytoplasm.

Next he uses a second needle to inject another, whole cell under the egg's outer layer. With the flip of an electric switch, the cloning is complete: the electrical pulse fuses the introduced cell to the egg, and the early embryo begins to divide. In a few days, it will become a mass of cells large enough to implant into the uterus of a surrogate-mother animal previously treated with hormones. In a matter of months, that surrogate mother will give birth to a clone.

In practice, though, this technique—which scientists call nuclear transfer—is not so easy. To create Noah, we at Advanced Cell Technology (ACT) in Worcester, Mass., had to fuse skin cells taken from a male gaur with 692 enucleated cow eggs. As we report in [a 2000] issue of the journal *Cloning*, of those 692 cloned early embryos, only 81 grew in the laboratory into blastocysts, balls of 100 or so cells that are sufficiently developed to implant for gestation. We ended up inserting 42 blastocysts into 32 cows, but only eight became pregnant. We removed the fetuses from two of the pregnant cows for scientific analysis; four other animals experienced spontaneous abortions in the second or third month of the usual nine-month pregnancy; and the seventh cow had a very unexpected late-term spontaneous abortion in August [2000]. . . .

## Determining the Species to Be Cloned

We expect that the first few endangered species to be cloned will be those whose reproduction has already been well studied. Several zoos and conservation societies—including the Audubon Institute Center for Research of Endangered Species (AICRES) in New Orleans—have probed the reproductive biology of a range of endangered species, with some notable successes. [In November 1999], for example, [Betsy L.] Dresser and her colleagues reported the first transplantation of a previously frozen embryo of an endangered animal into another species that resulted in a live birth. In this case, an ordinary house cat gave birth to an African wildcat, a species that has declined in some areas.

So far, beyond the African wildcat and the gaur, we and others have accomplished interspecies embryo transfers in four additional cases: an Indian desert cat into a domestic cat; a bongo antelope into a more common African antelope called an eland; a mouflon sheep into a domestic sheep; and a rare red deer into a common white-tailed deer.

All yielded live births. We hope that the studies of felines will pave the way for cloning the cheetah, of which only roughly 12,000 remain in southern Africa. The prolonged courtship behavior of cheetahs requires substantial territory, a possible explanation for why the animals have bred so poorly in zoos and yet another reason to fear their extinction as their habitat shrinks. . . .

*Some endangered animals such as the bongo antelope shown here have been successfully cloned.*

## An Important Preservation Tool

Cloning endangered species is controversial, but we assert that it has an important place in plans to manage species that are in danger of extinction. Some researchers have argued against it, maintaining that it would restrict an already dwindling amount of genetic diversity for those species. Not so. We advocate the establishment of a worldwide network of repositories to hold frozen tissue from all the individuals of an endangered species from which it is possible to collect samples. Those cells—like the sperm and eggs now being collected in "frozen zoos" by a variety of zoological parks—could serve as a genetic trust for reconstituting entire populations of a given species. Such an enterprise would be relatively inexpen-

*Embryos of animals such as the cheetah can be maintained for future cloning in "frozen zoos."*

*Leaders in animal cloning research such as Dr. X. Jerry Yang continue to refine the cloning process.*

sive: a typical three-foot freezer can hold more than 2,000 samples and uses just a few dollars of electricity per year. Currently only AICRES and the San Diego Zoo's Center for Reproduction of Endangered Species maintain banks of frozen body cells that could be used for cloning.

Other critics claim that the practice could overshadow efforts to preserve habitat. We counter that while habitat preservation is the keystone of species conservation, some countries are too poor or too unstable to support sustainable conservation efforts. What is more, the continued growth of the human species will probably make it impossible to save enough habitat for some other species. Cloning by interspecies nuclear transfer offers the possibility of keeping the genetic stock of those species on hand without maintaining populations in captivity, which is a particularly costly enterprise in the case of large animals.

Another argument against cloning endangered species is that it might siphon donor money away from habitat maintenance. But not all potential donors are willing to support efforts to stem the tide of habitat destruction. We should recognize that some who would otherwise not donate to preserve endangered species at all might want to support cloning or other assisted reproduction technologies.

The time to act is now.

## EVALUATING THE AUTHORS' ARGUMENTS:

The authors of the text you just read end their viewpoint by responding to the claims of critics who oppose cloning endangered species. Did they address the claims made by Malcolm Tait in the viewpoint that follows? Explain, citing from the texts.

# Cloning Does Not Promote the Conservation of Endangered Species

### Malcolm Tait

> "The cloning of endangered species is as far removed from the spirit and psychology of conservation as we've ever been."

Malcolm Tait claims in the following viewpoint that cloning is not the proper way to save endangered species. In fact, he contends, cloning is not about conservation but about humankind's desire to control the environment. Conservation is about reducing man's impact on the environment; thus saving endangered species requires sacrifices, Tait argues. However, if cloning becomes easier than saving a forest, for example, people will be less inclined to want to make those sacrifices, he maintains. At the time this viewpoint was written, Tait was managing editor of the *Ecologist*, a nonprofit environmental magazine that also leads environmental campaigns.

Malcolm Tait, "Bessie and the Gaur," *Ecologist,* December 2000. Copyright © 2000 by MIT Press Journals. Reproduced by permission.

**AS YOU READ, CONSIDER THE FOLLOWING QUESTIONS:**
1. In Tait's opinion, what is the central theme of environmental ethical arguments?
2. Why is conservation a precarious affair, in the authors' view?
3. According to the author, where might we put cloned creatures after their habitat is gone?

Mankind has always enjoyed testing its own limits, of course, and there's nothing it likes better than a good ethical argument—talk radio and TV chat shows wouldn't survive without it—but we've entered a moral maze [in 2000] that has heads spinning.

## A Moral Maze

As ever, the arguments boil down to one key confrontation: the needs of the planet versus the rights of the individual. The topic—genetics—may be comparatively new, but it's the same old argument. The world has more people than it can cater for: yes, but if science can help my childless marriage, why shouldn't I have the right to take advantage of it? Excessive vehicle use causes global warming and ultimately destruction: yes, but I need my car to get my children to school. The long-term prospects would appear to be disastrous: yes, but I need a short-term solution.

However, there's one of [2000's] genetic developments that has nothing to do with human rights, nothing to do, despite appearances to the contrary, with animal rights, and everything to do with scientific experimentation dressed up as benefit. [In December 2000], a cow named Bessie from Iowa was due to give birth to a gaur, an

Source: Kauffmann. © by Joel Kauffmann. Reproduced by permission.

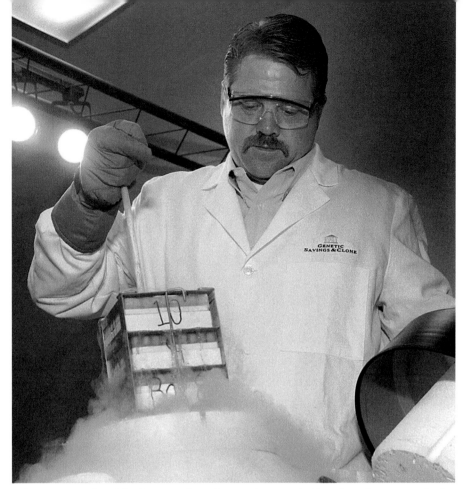

*Cloning researchers like this man from Genetic Savings & Clone have been accused of hampering species conservation efforts.*

endangered ox-like animal from Asia. The process was achieved by injecting gaur cells, complete with their DNA, into hollowed-out cow eggs, then electrically fusing the eggs and DNA together. Of the 81 successfully developed eggs that were implanted into cattle, eight resulted in pregnancy, three managed not to miscarry, and two turned into embryos which were removed for monitoring. Only Bessie soldiered on. At the time *The Ecologist* went to press, Bessie was still approaching labour, but whether or not this first experiment was successful, it won't be the last. [Bessie gave birth to Noah on January 8, 2001.]

Already there are plans afoot for more work along similar lines. The bucardo, a Pyrenean mountain goat, became extinct in January [2000], when the last of its kind was put out of its lonely misery by a falling tree. Cells were taken from the corpse, and the Massachusetts-based company Advanced Cell Technology is planning to clone the creature back to life. The panda is next on the list for rejuvenation, and there's talk of trying to bring back the Tasmanian tiger, a wolf-like animal that lost its last grip on survival in the 1930s. . . .

There's no doubt that the thought of bringing back the bucardo, an extinct species, certainly stimulates the imagination. It's a fascinating scientific gimmick, a perfect example of doing something because we can. We should leave it at that.

## Cloning Is Not the Spirit of Conservation

But we won't. Already there is talk of this process being a marvellous aid to conservation, a boon to the world's endangered species, a solution to the perennial problem of man's cohabitation with beast. This is tripe, for the cloning of endangered species is as far removed from the spirit and psychology of conservation as we've ever been since man first noticed he was killing off the birds and beasts.

Conservation is a precarious affair, because its failure is finite. It has, quite literally, a deadline. Sometimes that deadline is easy to see, other times it's not. In the 1980s, it was realised that whales were struggling in their relationship with man, and new laws and consumption restrictions were put into place. By the early 1990s, the plight of the elephant came to life, and reasonably successfully dealt with. We've recently discovered that the troubled tiger is in even more danger than we'd previously thought. Wheels are beginning to turn. Yet for every headline species that captures the heart, there are many many more that don't make it. Most of the world first heard of Miss Waldron's Red Colobus monkey this year [2000], for example, when it was announced that it had become extinct. A sense of simultaneous gain and loss.

Extinction, of course, is part of evolution, and had man's footprint not covered the lands and seas, the world would still have continued its course of saying farewell to species whose day had gone. The fact is, however, that man has not just accelerated that process, but is continuing to do so at a rate that doesn't allow the surviving species to adjust to their new ecosystems. Conservation isn't just about saving a particular species, it's about reducing our destructive impact on natural processes that are in increasing danger of being unable to sustain themselves, and ultimately, therefore, of sustaining us.

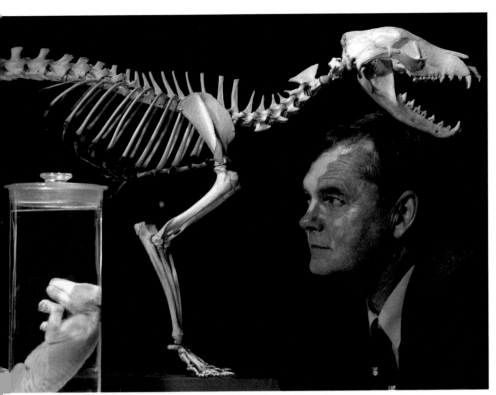

*Opponents fear that if scientists were to clone extinct species such as the Tasmanian tiger (embryo and skeleton pictured), the destruction of wildlife and habitat would continue unabated.*

There's too much at stake, for nature and for ourselves, to take conservation lightly. But conservation takes time and money. It requires careful management and planning, and involves apparent sacrifices. It demands that the long-term view takes precedence over, or is at least built into, the short term. If conservation is going to work, mankind has to want it so much that it hurts.

## A Slippery Slope

Which brings us back to Bessie. Suddenly, for the first time ever, we've got an alternative to conservation. It's only a tiny crack at present, but science will want to widen it. What's the point in putting all that effort into looking after ecosystems if we've got the ability to clone everything back into existence? Just think of what we can achieve—we can carry on crashing through the planet, doing what we want, and whenever some species starts to totter as a result, we've got the technology to see it through the

*Rather than clone endangered animals, conservationists believe the most effective way to save endangered species, such as the Indian elephant, Zanzibar red colobus monkey (right), and the tiger (far right), from extinction is to protect their habitats.*

hard times. Of course, no biotech company would put it like that at present—it would appear as scientific coldheartedness and therefore be commercial suicide—but the option will be there. Cloning endangered species is a classic case of science no longer being used for prevention, but for apparent cure. It is lazy science. However much its supporters may protest that cloning will only ever be used to complement conservation, to step in when conservation has failed, the day will come when the financial benefits of, say, clearing a forest will outweigh the costs of cloning the endangered species within. Someone will be prepared to pay for it, and the rot will have begun.

But what will we then do with these phoenix-like creatures? If their habitat is no more, where will we put them? Perhaps we will create reservations for them—but to save space, we'll need to make sure we only hang on to the species which benefit ourselves. We'll need to recreate habitats that suit them, and if our new cloned versions require special diets, or develop viruses or illnesses that their originals never encountered, then we can genetically modify their surroundings to suit. Any imperfections that are built in, we can decode and correct. In short, who needs Nature's ecosystems, when we can create our own?

This may seem a far-fetched future, but it is in fact perfectly in line with the way mankind has always been—except that he's now taking a bigger step than ever before. . . . Why would anyone think he wouldn't instinctively want to go that one further step—albeit a mightier one than ever—and restructure nature to suit his precise needs?

## Passing the Buck

None of this is to say that genetic scientists and those who fund them are necessarily power-mad, corrupt seekers of world domination. Science is the discipline of discovery, of finding out, of increasing knowledge. Thus it is that, generally, each new step forward is taken with the honest and sincere desire to benefit man. Yet it's curious how often genetic scientists, nudging the process onward, tend to see their own work in isolation and distinct from the overall movement. . . .

Ultimately, we should none of us be fooled. The cloning of endangered or extinct animals is an extraordinary feat, and one which, if continued, will inevitably lead to yet more and more extraordinary feats.

It is the latest stage in man's attempts to control his world, and like Frankenstein's monster, it may one day lead to its creator's own destruction.

So let's drop the pretence right now. Let's honestly admit to ourselves what we're getting into. Cloning is a brand-new chapter in the history of mankind, but it has nothing, absolutely nothing, to do with conservation.

### EVALUATING THE AUTHORS' ARGUMENTS:

In the viewpoint you just read, what type of evidence does Malcolm Tait use to support his claim that cloning does not promote conservation? Is this evidence more or less convincing than the evidence used by the authors of the previous viewpoint? Explain, citing from the viewpoints.

# GLOSSARY

**adult stem cell:** A cell found in the body tissue of an adult organism. Adult stem cells are **undifferentiated**, which means that they have not yet received the signal to perform a specific function such as a blood, nerve, or muscle cell. These cells can renew themselves until they are needed to perform a specific function.

**asexual reproduction:** Reproduction that is accomplished by a process other than the fertilization of an egg by a sperm. The genetic material in asexual reproduction comes from one organism rather than from both a male and female organism.

**blastocyst:** A fertilized egg in the early stages of development that consists of a ball of about thirty to fifty cells. The inner mass of cells will become the fetus, and the outer ring of cells will become part of the placenta, which envelops the fetus and is attached to the mother's womb.

**cell line:** A term applied to a collection of cells that has been maintained in a laboratory for an extended period. These cells continue to divide and replicate themselves and are used in experiments.

**chromosomes:** Long pieces of **DNA** located inside the nucleus of a cell that are duplicated each time the cell divides. Chromosomes transmit the genes of an organism from one generation to the next.

**clone:** 1) An exact genetic replica of a **DNA** molecule, cell, tissue, organ, or entire plant or animal. 2) An organism that has the same genetic make-up as another organism.

**cloned embryo:** An embryo that has been created by **somatic cell nuclear transfer** (SCNT) rather than by the union of a sperm and an egg. SCNT involves inserting the nucleus of a body cell into an egg from which the nucleus has been removed. The egg is then stimulated to develop into an embryo.

**cloning:** The process of creating a living organism or embryo that is genetically identical to an already existing or previously existing individual.

**culture:** The growth of cells, tissues, or embryos in a laboratory.

**cytoplasm:** The contents of a cell other than the nucleus. Cytoplasm consists of a fluid that contains structures known as organelles that carry out the functions of the cell.

**differentiation:** In cells, the process of changing from the kind of cell that can develop into any part of the body, called an **undifferentiated** cell, to a specialized cell such as a blood, nerve, or muscle cell.

**DNA:** A chemical, deoxyribonucleic acid, found primarily in the nucleus of cells. DNA is the genetic material that contains the instructions for making all the structures and materials the body needs to function. Chromosomes and their subunits, genes, are made up primarily of DNA.

**embryo:** 1) The developing organism from the time of fertilization until a significant number of cells have specialized into body tissue cells and when the organism then becomes known as a fetus. 2) An organism in the early stages of development.

**embryonic stem cells:** The cells of an embryo that have not yet received the chemical signal to become specialized cells. These cells are called **pluripotent** because they have the potential to become a wide variety of specialized cell types.

**embryo splitting** or **twinning:** The separation of an early-stage embryo into two or more embryos with identical genetic makeup, essentially creating identical twins, triplets, or quadruplets, etc.

**enucleated egg:** An egg cell whose nucleus has been removed or destroyed.

**eugenics:** An attempt to alter the genetic constitution of future generations with the aim of improving it.

**gamete:** A reproductive cell such as an egg or a sperm cell that has only one-half of the chromosomes needed to form an organism.

**gene:** A genetic unit of **DNA** located at a specific site on a chromosome.

**genome:** The complete genetic material of an organism.

**germ cells** or **germ line cells:** Reproductive cells such as a sperm, an egg, or a cell that can develop into a sperm or egg; all other body cells are called **somatic cells.**

**in vitro fertilization (IVF):** The fertilization of an egg by a sperm in an artificial environment outside the body. The term *in vitro* means, literally, "in glass"; in a test tube, for example.

**mitochondria:** A cellular organ called an organelle that provides the energy the cell needs to live. It contains some genetic material, the genetic information needed to keep the cell going, and enzymes that convert food into energy.

**multipotent cell:** A cell that can produce several different types of **differentiated** cells, which are cells that perform a specific function in the body such as blood, nerve, or muscle cells.

**nonsomatic cells:** Cells that are used for reproduction, such as a sperm or an egg cell. They contain only half of an organism's chromosomes.

**nuclear transfer:** A procedure in which the nucleus from a donor cell is transferred into an egg from which the nucleus has been removed. The donor nucleus can come from **germ** (reproductive) **cells** or **somatic** (body) **cells.**

**nucleus:** A cellular organ that contains all of the cell's genes except those found in the mitochondria, the energy-producing organ of the cell.

**oocyte:** The developing female reproductive cell (the developing egg) that is produced in a female organism's ovaries.

**organism:** Any living individual, whole animal.

**pluripotent:** A cell that can give rise to many different types of specialized cells. A pluripotent cell, after receiving a chemical signal, can become nearly any type of tissue such as a heart, brain, or a muscle.

**somatic cells:** All cells that are not reproductive (sperm or egg) cells. Somatic (body) cells have a complete set of chromosomes while reproductive cells have only half.

**somatic cell nuclear transfer (SCNT):** The transfer of the nucleus from a donor somatic (body) cell into an egg from which the nucleus has been removed in order to produce a cloned embryo.

**stem cells:** Cells that are called **undifferentiated** because they have not yet become **differentiated,** which means that they have not yet been given the chemical signal to become specialized cells such as blood, nerve, or muscle cells. These cells can, however, replicate themselves until they become **differentiated**, or specialized.

**totipotent:** A cell that can develop into any kind of cell, which in turn develops into a complete adult organism and its tissues.

**undifferentiated:** A type of cell that has not yet received the chemical signal to serve a specific function such as a blood, nerve, or muscle cell. These cells can become almost any type of cell once they receive the chemical signal to do so.

**zygote:** The cell that results from the fertilization of an egg cell by a sperm cell. As a result, this cell has a complete set of **chromosomes**.

# FACTS ABOUT CLONING

Editor's Note: These facts can be used in reports or papers to reinforce or add credibility when making important points or claims.

## What Is Cloning?

Cloning is the transplantation of a nucleus from a body cell into an egg cell from which the nucleus has been removed. The process is called somatic cell nuclear transfer (SCNT). The cell then develops into an embryo. The embryo is an exact genetic copy of the organism whose somatic cell nucleus was injected into the egg. What happens after this process determines the specific type of cloning.

## Reproductive Cloning Versus Therapeutic Cloning

- If the goal is to create a new organism by planting the cloned embryo into the uterus of an adult female, the process is called reproductive cloning.
- If the goal is to harvest stem cells from the cloned embryo to grow tissues and other biological products with therapeutic value, the process is called therapeutic cloning.

## The Cloning of Dolly the Sheep

On February 22, 1997, scientists Ian Wilmut and Keith Campbell at the Roslin Institute in Edinburgh, Scotland, announced that they had cloned the first mammal from the cell of an adult sheep. Wilmut and Campbell named the lamb Dolly. To create Dolly, they used the somatic cell nuclear transfer (SCNT) cloning process. The scientists first obtained cells with nuclear material, in which genetic information is coded. Wilmut and Campbell used cells from the frozen mammary tissue of a six-year-old Finn Dorset ewe. They next obtained a sheep egg cell and removed its nucleus. This egg was fused with the mammary tissue cells in a petri dish and subjected to an electric current. The donor cell and egg were fused into a fertilized egg. After growing and dividing for a week or so in the laboratory, the fused cell formed into an early-stage embryo called a blastocyst. Wilmut's team implanted the blastocyst into surrogate mothers. Out of 277 such implantations only one lamb, Dolly, was born.

## What Constitutes a Human Clone?

A human clone is a genetic identical twin. It is created from the nuclear material of a donor, which is then fused with an egg cell from which the nucleus has been removed. The developing "cloned" egg begins to develop and is then planted into a surrogate womb, where it develops and is born as it would if it had been fertilized by a sperm. A human clone would be a generation or more younger than its twin, who would provide the nucleus from which the clone would be created. The mother who gives birth to the clone provides none of a clone's DNA. Because people are more than a product of their genes, most analysts agree that a clone would have its own personality, character, intelligence, and talents, just like identical twins. Thus, even if people wanted to, they could not duplicate themselves exactly. They could only duplicate their physical characteristics, and even these would vary somewhat as a result of environmental influences: diet, exercise, and injuries, for example. Thus many believe that every human life, no matter how conceived, is unique.

## Adult Stem Cells and Embryonic Stem Cells

Stem cells differ from other kinds of cells in the body. A stem cell is an undifferentiated cell, one that has not yet developed into a cell that serves a special function in the body. After receiving a chemical signal, the undifferentiated cell develops into a specialized cell such as a blood, nerve, or muscle cell. All stem cells have three characteristics:

- They are capable of dividing and renewing themselves for long periods.
- They are unspecialized, meaning they have not yet developed a specific function in the body.
- They can give rise to specialized cell types, which do have a function in the body.

**Stem cells can come from two different sources:**

- Adult stem cells are undifferentiated cells found in the body. The primary role of adult stem cells in a living organism is to maintain and repair the tissue in which it is found. Some people believe that adult stem cells, after being given the signal to perform a specific function, can replace diseased or dysfunctional cells with healthy, functioning ones. In fact, scientists have been able to persuade blood stem cells to behave like neurons or brain cells. They hope that further research on adult stem cell therapy may cure diseases such as diabetes, Alzheimer's and Parkinson's, degenerative diseases in which the cells of the tissue no longer function properly. Those who support adult stem cell research believe that adult stem cells should be used instead of embryonic stem cells in which the embryo is destroyed to obtain the stem cells.

- Embryonic stem cells have the same characteristics as adult stem cells but come from human embryos instead of the body itself. They develop from eggs that have been fertilized in vitro, an artifical environment outside the womb such as a laboratory dish or test tube. Some scientists believe that embryonic stem cells have more potential as a cure for degenerative diseases because embryonic stem cells can develop into a greater number of cell types while the cell types an adult stem cell can become are more limited. Scientists claim that they can exert greater control over how embryonic stem cells will function in the body. Some scientists hope to someday obtain embryonic stem cells from cloned embryos. (See therapeutic cloning below.) They contend that this research is the best hope for those with degenerative diseases.

## How Might Therapeutic Cloning Cure Debilitating Diseases?

Brain injuries, heart failure, and diseases such as diabetes, Parkinson's, and Alzheimer's have one thing in common: They involve the loss of specialized cells that the body cannot replace on its own. This cell depletion is the root cause of these and many other diseases. So far, only the symptoms of these diseases can be treated. There are no cures. However, researchers hope to cultivate and replace these lost tissue cells.

Every cell in the body has the same collection of approximately twenty-five thousand genes. Different genes are active in different types of cells. This genetic activity is what makes a heart cell different from a brain or a kidney cell. A stem cell in a five-day-old embryo could develop into any of these specialized cell types, but this pluripotent state does not last very long. The stem cell picks up chemical signals from its surroundings. Different genes get switched on or silenced, and the cell then becomes specialized. Once specialized, these cells can no longer switch their roles, and few are able to reproduce. Thus when a person has a heart attack or a brain injury, the organs cannot repair themselves.

Some scientists believe that embryonic stem cell therapy could change that, but scientists first had to learn how cells develop and specialize. For example, which cells will activate the nerve cell that manufactures dopamine, the chemical that victims of Parkinson's lack? Scientists have already used stem cells to treat Parkinson's, diabetes, and spinal-cord injuries in mice. Most researchers agree that the same therapy will work on people. However, the most reliable source of high-quality pluripotent stem cells for use in humans are human embryos. The supply is limited, and the process is controversial.

Several researchers believe that therapeutic cloning is the answer. Therapeutic cloning could provide people with their own supply of embryonic stem cells. The nucleus of a person's body cell could be injected into a human egg cell from which the nucleus has been removed. This cell would then divide and develop into a two hundred–cell embryo from which one's own stem cells could be extracted. Because these were one's own cells, they would not be rejected by the body, a problem anticipated by using cells from in vitro fertilization clinics.

**Advanced Cell Technology**
381 Plantation St., Biotech Five, Worcester, MA 01605
(508) 756-1212
fax: (508) 756-4468
Web site: www.advancedcell.com

Advanced Cell Technology, Inc. is a leading biotechnology company in the emerging field of regenerative medicine. Its focus is on cloning technology for the production of young cells for the treatment of cell degenerative diseases. Its Web site provides links to many scientific articles on cloning.

**American Life League (ALL)**
PO Box 1350, Stafford, VA 22555
(540) 659-4171
fax: (540) 659-2586
e-mail: jbrown@all.org
Web site: www.all.org

ALL is an educational pro-life organization that opposes abortion, artificial contraception, reproductive technologies, and fetal experimentation. It asserts that it is immoral to perform experiments on living human embryos and fetuses, whether inside or outside the mother's womb. Its publications include the bimonthly magazine *Celebrate Life*, the fact sheet "Adult Stem Cell Research Successes," and the white paper "Broken Promises."

**American Medical Association (AMA)**
515 N. State St., Chicago, IL 60610
(800) 621-8335
Web site: www.ama-assn.org

The AMA is the largest and most prestigious professional association for medical doctors. It helps set standards for medical education and practices and is a powerful lobby in Washington for physicians' interests. The association publishes monthly journals for many medical fields as well as the weekly *JAMA* and the report *The Ethics of Cloning.*

**Americans to Ban Cloning (ABC)**
Web site: www.cloninginformation.org

ABC is a coalition of organizations and individuals whose goal is to promote a comprehensive, global ban on cloning. It believes human cloning would commodify life and result in a race of second-class citizens. Its Web site offers a variety of articles, commentaries, and congressional testimony against human cloning.

**Audubon Nature Institute's Center for Research of Endangered Species**
PO Box 4327, New Orleans, LA 70178
(504) 861-2537
e-mail: air@auduboninstitute.org
Web site: www.auduboninstitute.org/rcenter

The Center for Research of Endangered Species at the Audubon Nature Institute studies reproductive physiology, endocrinology, genetics, and nuclear embryo transfer (cloning) to cope with threats to the most seriously endangered species. Its "frozen zoo," a bank of genetic materials, hopes to ensure the future of endangered species. On its Web site the center publishes fact sheets on research areas and publishes the institute's annual "Conservation Report."

**BC Biotechnology Alliance (BCBA)**
1122 Mainland St., #450, Vancouver, BC V6B 5L1 Canada
(604) 689-5602
fax: (604) 689-5603
Web site: www.biotech.pc.ca/bcba

The BCBA is an association for producers and users of biotechnology. The alliance works to increase public awareness and understanding of biotechnology, including the awareness of its potential contributions to society. The alliance's publications include the bimonthly newsletter *Biofax* and the annual *Directory of BC Biotechnology Capabilities.*

**Biotechnology Industry Organization (BIO)**
1225 Eye St. NW, Suite 400, Washington, DC 20005
(202) 962-9200

fax: (202) 962-9201
e-mail: biomember@bio.org
Web site: www.bio.org

BIO represents biotechnology companies, academic institutions, state biotechnology centers, and related organizations that support the use of biotechnology in improving health care, agriculture, efforts to clean up the environment, and other fields. BIO works to educate the public about biotechnology and respond to concerns about the safety of genetic engineering and other technologies. It publishes *Bioethics: Facing the Future Responsibly* and an introductory guide to biotechnology, which are available on its Web site.

**The Center for Bioethics and Human Dignity**
2065 Half Day Rd. Bannockburn, IL 60015
(847) 317-8180
fax: (847) 317-8101
e-mail: info@cbhd.org
Web site: www.cbhd.org

The Center for Bioethics and Human Dignity is an international education center whose purpose is to bring Christian perspectives to bear on contemporary bioethical challenges facing society. Its publications address human cloning and stem cell research as well as other topics in genetic technology. It publishes the newsletter *Dignity* and the policy statement "Human Cloning: The Need for a Comprehensive Ban."

**Clone Rights United Front/Clone Rights Action Center**
506 Hudson St., New York, NY 10014
(212) 255-1439
fax: (212) 463-0435
e-mail: r.wicker@verizon.net
Web site: www.clonerights.org

The Clone Rights United Front began as a one-issue reproductive rights organization. It was organized to oppose legislation that would make cloning a human being a felony. It is dedicated to the principle that reproductive rights, including cloning, are guaranteed by the Constitution, and that each citizen has the right to decide if, when, and how to reproduce. Its Web site has links to congressional testimony opposing a ban on human cloning and editorials supporting cloning.

**Coalition for the Advancement of Medical Research (CAMR)**
2120 L St. NW, Suite 850, Washington, DC 20037
(202) 833-0355
e-mail: CAMResearch@yahoo.com
Web site: www.camradvocacy.org

CAMR is comprised of nationally recognized patient organizations, universities, scientific societies, foundations, and individuals with life-threatening illnesses and disorders who advocate for the advancement of breakthrough research and technologies in regenerative medicine—including stem cell research and somatic cell nuclear transfer—in order to cure disease and alleviate suffering. The coalition believes embryonic stem cell research must remain a legal and protected form of scientific research. Its Web site offers a variety of links to press releases, editorials, and Congressional testimony in support of its views.

**The Genetics and Public Policy Center**
1717 Massachusetts Ave. NW, Suite 530, Washington, DC 20036
(202) 663-5971
fax: (202) 663-5992
e-mail: inquiries@DNApolicy.org
Web site: www.DNApolicy.org

The Genetics and Public Policy Center was established as an independent and objective source of credible information on genetic technologies and genetic policies for the public, media, and policy makers. The center undertakes public opinion polls concerning reproductive genetic technology and its Web site includes the article "The Regulatory Environment for Human Cloning."

**Genetic Savings & Clone, Inc. (GSC)**
(888) 833-6063
fax: (415) 289-2526
Web site: www.savingsandclone.com

GSC is a company that clones pets and serves as a bank for pet genes. In 2003, GSC announced its "Nine Lives Extravaganza," the world's first commercial cat cloning service. GSC publishes a cloning newsletter, *The Dish*. Available on the GSC Web site are articles about cloning, its social benefits, and the pet cloning debate, including "Cloning

Companion Animals Is Wrong," "New Dog: Old Tricks," and GSC CEO Lou Hawthorne's rebuttal to these articles.

**The Hastings Center**
21 Malcolm Gordon Rd., Garrison NY 10524-5555
(845) 424-4040
fax: (845) 424-4545
e-mail: mail@thehastingscenter.org
Web site: www.thehastingscenter.org

This research institute addresses fundamental ethical issues in health, medicine, and the environment, including issues related to genetics and human cloning. The center publishes books, papers, guidelines, and the bimonthly *Hastings Center Report,* which has published several articles on cloning.

**National Institutes of Health (NIH)**
9000 Rockville Pike, Bethesda, MD 20892
(301) 496-4000
Web site: www.nih.gov

The NIH is the federal government's primary agency for the support of biomedical research. It is the government agency responsible for developing guidelines for research on stem cells. Its Web site includes numerous links to articles about stem cell research and frequently asked questions.

**Patients' Coalition for Urgent Research (CURe)**
Alliance for Aging Research
2021 K St. NW, Suite 305, Washington, DC 20006
(202) 293-2856
fax: (202) 785-8574
Web site: www.agingresearch.org

CURe is a coalition of more than thirty patient advocacy and disease groups under the leadership of the Alliance for Aging Research. It is an active federal funding lobby for embryo and stem cell research. CURe believes that science can help people live longer, more productive lives.

**People for the Ethical Treatment of Animals (PETA)**
501 Front St., Norfolk, VA 23510
(757) 622-7382
Web site: www.peta-online.org

PETA is an educational and activist group that opposes all forms of animal exploitation, including cloning. It conducts rallies and demonstrations to focus attention on animal experimentation, the fur fashion industry, and the killing of animals for human consumption. PETA hopes to educate the public about attitudes toward animals and about the conditions in slaughterhouses and research laboratories. It publishes reports on these issues in the quarterly newsletter *Animal Times*. On its Web site PETA publishes news and articles on pet cloning, including "Put the Kibosh on Cat Cloning."

### President's Council on Bioethics
1801 Pennsylvania Ave. NW, Suite 700, Washington, DC 20006
(202) 296-4669
e-mail: info@bioethics.gov
Web site: www.bioethics.gov

The council was formed by an executive order in 2001 to advise the president on bioethical issues as a result of emerging biotechnology. In addition, the council explores ethical and policy questions and provides a forum for a national discussion of these issues. Its reports include the books *Human Cloning and Human Dignity: An Ethical Inquiry*, and *Being Human: Readings from the President's Council on Bioethics*.

# FOR FURTHER READING

## Books

Andrea L. Bonnicksen, *Crafting a Cloning Policy: From Dolly to Stem Cells.* Washington, DC: Georgetown University Press, 2002. A political science professor examines the political responses to advances in cloning and embryonic stem cell research, discussing international, federal, and state laws.

Holly Cefrey, *Cloning and Genetic Engineering.* Danbury, CT: Children's Press, 2002. An overview of the technological and social issues surrounding cloning and genetic engineering, including a look at what the future of cloning might bring.

Karl Drlica, *Understanding DNA and Gene Cloning: A Guide for the Curious.* Hoboken, NJ: Wiley, 2004. Provides an introductory examination of the science and technology of genetic engineering, including cloning.

Jeanne DuPrau, *Cloning.* San Diego, CA: Lucent Books, 2000. Discusses the methods, regulation, and ethics of cloning as used in agriculture and medicine and endangered species and human beings.

Francis Fukuyama, *Our Posthuman Future: Consequences of the Biotechnology Revolution.* New York: Farrar, Straus and Giroux, 2002. Explores potential threats posed by biotechnology, including genetic engineering, and suggests methods to regulate it.

Walter Glannon, *Genes and Future People: Philosophical Issues in Human Genetics.* Boulder, CO: Westview Press, 2001. The author believes that cloning is morally permissible if used for therapeutic goals, but he urges caution.

David Goodnough, *The Debate over Human Cloning.* Berkeley Heights, NJ: Enslow, 2003. Provides an overview of the technology and history of cloning and arguments for and against human cloning.

S. Holland, K. Lebacqz, and L. Zoloth, eds., *The Human Embryonic Stem Cell Debate: Science, Ethics and Public Policy.* Cambridge, MA: MIT Press, 2001. Explores the science of human embryonic stem cell research and differing views on the ethical issues it raises.

Arleen Judith Klotzko, *The Cloning Sourcebook.* New York: Oxford University Press, 2001. Prominent participants in the cloning debate present their viewpoints on recent developments, popular misconceptions, ethical concerns, and proposed regulations.

John Charles Kunich, *The Naked Clone: How Cloning Bans Threaten Our Personal Rights.* Westport, CT: Praeger, 2003. A law professor contends that banning therapeutic and reproductive cloning would violate Americans' rights to personal autonomy, privacy, reproduction, and freedom of expression.

Glenn McGee, *The Perfect Baby: Parenthood in the New World of Cloning and Genetics.* 2nd ed. Lanham, MD: Rowman & Littlefield, 2000. Explores ethical issues in high-tech reproduction, including gene therapy, cloning, and stem cell research.

Glenn McGee, ed., *The Human Cloning Debate.* 2nd ed. Berkeley, CA: Berkeley Hills Books, 2000. Lawyers, molecular scientists, and ethicists discuss cloning history, technology, policy, and ethics. Several different religions are represented in the discussion.

Bill McKibben, *Enough: Staying Human in an Engineered Age.* New York: Times Books, 2003. Argues that genetic engineering advances should be regulated because they may change what it means to be human.

Gregory E. Pence, *Flesh of My Flesh: The Ethics of Cloning Humans. A Reader.* Lanham, MD: Rowman & Littlefield, 1998. Philosophers, bioethicists, religious leaders, and scientists comment upon the reproductive cloning of human beings.

Gregory E. Pence, *Who's Afraid of Human Cloning?* New York: Rowman & Littlefield, 1998. The author argues that people should not fear cloning but consider it another reproductive option.

Ted Peters, *Playing God? Genetic Determinism and Human Freedom.* New York: Taylor & Francis, 2003. Expresses the view that human beings are more than their genes and the dangers of this myth. Cloning chapters explain that human clones, although genetically identical, would be distinct individuals and that God's grace, not DNA, determines one's relationship to God.

Ray Spangenburg and Kit Moser, *Genetic Engineering.* New York: Benchmark Books, 2004. Discusses the science and the controversy surrounding the use of genetic engineering in plants and animals.

Gregory Stock, *Redesigning Humans: Our Inevitable Genetic Future.* Boston: Houghton Mifflin, 2002. Argues that the genetic engineering of children to protect them from disease and improve their looks and abilities is inevitable and attempts to control it will be futile.

Ian Wilmut, Keith Campbell, and Colin Tudge, *The Second Creation: Dolly and the Age of Biological Control.* New York: Farrar, Straus and Giroux, 2000. Ian Wilmut and Keith Campbell, co-creators of Dolly the cloned sheep, discuss the history and science of cloning Dolly and other cloning projects. The authors express their opposition to human cloning.

## Periodicals and Reports

*Applied Genetics News,* "Cloning: Bringing Back Endangered Species," October 2000.

Hilary Bok, "Cloning Companion Animals Is Wrong," *Journal of Applied Animal Welfare Science,* 2002.

Lawrence I. Bonchek, "Stem Cells, Embryos, and Casualties of War," *Free Inquiry,* Summer 2002.

Thomas W. Clark, "Playing God, Carefully," *Humanist,* May 2000.

Eric Cohen, "New Genetics, Old Quandaries: Debating the Biotech Utopia," *Weekly Standard,* April 22, 2002.

Sally Deneen, "Designer People," *E,* January 2001.

Kyla Dunn, "Cloning Trevor," *Atlantic,* June 2002.

*Economist,* "Baby Steps," January 3, 2004.

Anthony Faiola, "Dr. Clone: Creating Life or Trying to Save It?" *Washington Post,* February 29, 2004.

Thomas Fields-Meyer and Debbie Seaman, "Send In the Clones," *People,* September 8, 2003.

Laurie Goodstein and Denise Grady, "Split on Clones of Embryos: Research vs. Reproduction," *New York Times,* February 13, 2004.

Mark Greene, "New Dog: Old Tricks," *Journal of Applied Animal Welfare Science,* 2002.

Stephen Hall, "Specter of Cloning May Prove a Mirage," *New York Times,* February 17, 2004.

Brian Hanson, "Cloning Debate," *CQ Researcher*, October 22, 2004.

Daniel Henninger, "'Stop!'" *Wall Street Journal*, February 27, 2004.

Deal W. Hudson, "Stem Cells Equal Baby Parts," *Crisis*, May 2000.

*Issues and Controversies*, "Human Cloning," May 23, 2004.

William F. Jasper, "Latest Assault on the Preborn," *New American*, August 27, 2001.

Gina Kolata, "Cloning Creates Human Embryos," *New York Times*, February 12, 2004.

Gregory Lamb, "In Cloning Debate, a Compromise," *Christian Science Monitor*, April 8, 2004.

Stephen Leahy, "Biotech Hope and Hype," *Maclean's*, September 30, 2002.

B.J. Lee, "Cloning College," *Newsweek*, March 1, 2004.

Michael D. Lemonich, "Cloning Gets Closer," *Time*, February 23, 2004.

Celeste McGovern, "Brave New World," *Report Newsmagazine*, August 20, 2001.

Gilbert Meilaender, "Spare Embryos: If They're Going to Die Anyway, Does That Really Entitle Us to Treat Them as Handy Research Material?" *Weekly Standard*, August 26–September 2, 2002.

Pat Mooney, "Making Well People 'Better,'" *WorldWatch*, July/August 2002.

Wayne Pacelle, "Is Animal Cloning Ethical?" *San Francisco Chronicle*, January 21, 2005.

Andrew Pollack, "Cloning and Stem Cells: The Research," *New York Times*, February 18, 2004.

President's Council on Bioethics, "Human Cloning and Human Dignity: An Ethical Inquiry," July 2002.

Paul Raeburn et al., "Everything You Need to Know About Cloning," *Business Week*, April 29, 2002.

John A. Robertson, "Ethics and Policy in Embryonic Stem Cell Research," *Kennedy Institute of Ethics Journal*, June 1999.

Margot Roosevelt, "Stem-Cell Rebels," *Time*, May 17, 2004.

Edward Rothstein, "The Meaning of 'Human' in Embryonic Research," *New York Times*, March 13, 2004.

Carolyn Said, "$10 Million Bengal Kittens Pave Way for Pet Cloning," *San Francisco Chronicle*, August 6, 2004.

Peter Singer, "Stem Cells and Immortal Souls," *Free Inquiry*, Spring 2000.

Simon Smith, "Making Babies Ain't What It Used to Be," July 21, 2003. www.betterhumans.com.

Wesley J. Smith, "Is Bioethics Ethical?" *Weekly Standard*, April 3, 2000.

Betsy Streisand and Nell Boyce, "Stepping Up for Stem Cells," *U.S. News & World Report*, November 15, 2004.

Luba Vangelova, "True or False? Extinction Is Forever," *Smithsonian*, June 2003.

Dan Vregano, "States Dive into Stem Cell Debates," *USA Today*, April 21, 2004.

Robert A. Weinberg, "Of Clones and Clowns," *Atlantic Monthly*, June 2002.

Rick Weiss, "Stem Cells an Unlikely Therapy for Alzheimer's," *Washington Post*, June 10, 2004.

Sylvia Pagan Westphal, "Copy and Save," *New Scientist*, June 19–25, 2004.

## Web Sites

**Betterhumans.com** (www.betterhumans.com). Betterhumans.com explores and advocates the use of science and technology for furthering human progress. The Web site's cloning link includes articles and commentary on cloning, including "Cloned Stem Cells Fix Heart Muscle" and "Cloning Reverses Cancer."

**Clonaid** (www.clonaid.com). Clonaid was founded in 1997 by Rael, the spiritual leader of the Raelian Movement, the world's largest UFO-related organization. Clonaid is the first company to publicly announce its attempt to clone human beings. Clonaid believes that once human cloning has been perfected, the next step is to transfer memories and personalities into the newly cloned human brain, thus allowing a person to live forever. Clonaid and Rael have published the book *Yes to Human Cloning*, which examines why cloning is a feasible science. The Web site provides current articles and commentary supporting Clonaid's views.

**The Clone Zone** (www.bbc.co.uk/science/genes/gene_safari/clone_zone/intro.shtml). A British Broadcasting Corporation Web site, The Clone Zone tells the history and science of cloning, with articles on human, pet, agricultural animal, and endangered species cloning.

**Human Cloning Foundation** (www.humancloning.org). The foundation promotes education, awareness, and research about human cloning and other forms of biotechnology. It emphasizes the positive aspects of these new technologies. Its Web site offers a variety of resources, including essays on the benefits of human cloning and an online newsletter, *The Cloner.*

**The Reproductive Cloning Network** (www.ReproductiveCloning.net). The Reproductive Cloning Network provides information on reproductive and therapeutic human cloning. Articles included on the Web site support, oppose, or are neutral on the issue of cloning. Most articles, however, are in favor of cloning, including "Cloning Is Moral" and "Human Cloning Misconceptions." The Web site also provides links to other resources and commentary.

**Stem Clone Digest** (http://stemcellsclub.com/SCCC-homesite/stem clonedigest/index.html). Stem Clone Digest is an online journal that covers issues concerning regenerative medicine. Its primary emphasis is on stem cell, cloning, and cell therapy research. The Web site contains interviews, recent news, articles, and commentary, including "The Cloning Publicity Game" and "The Cloning of the Dead."

# INDEX

# PICTURE CREDITS

Cover: © CORBIS SYGMA
Maury Aaseng, 31, 75
AP/Wide World Photos, 12, 13,
    25, 37, 39, 42 (inset), 60, 65,
    72, 81, 84, 101, 107, 111
© Corel Corporation, 42, 114
EPA/Landov, 98
© Ronnen Eshel/CORBIS, 39
© Najlah Feanny/SABA/
    CORBIS, 35
© Al Francekevich/CORBIS, 21
Getty Images, 50
David Gray/Reuters/Landov, 113
Manuela Hartling/Reuters/
    Landov, 36
© Martin Harvey/CORBIS, 115
Sandy Huffaker/Getty Images, 76
Hwang Woo-Suk/UPI/Landov, 28
© Images.com/CORBIS, 20, 59
© Kim Kulish/CORBIS, 90
Daniele La Monaca/Reuters/
    Landov, 46

Lee Hoon-Gu/Getty Images, 9
Lee Jae-Won/Reuters/Landov,
    14, 18
© Joe McDonald/CORBIS, 92
Jeff J. Mitchell/Reuters/Landov,
    82
Miguel Angel Molina/EPA/
    Landov, 62
National Archives, 30
National Geographic/Getty
    Images, 105
Photos.com, 66, 102, 115
© RBM Online/Handout/
    Reuters/CORBIS, 10
© Reuters/CORBIS, 86
Reuters/Landov, 53, 95
Sydney IVF/EPA/Landov, 49
Tim Vernon, LTH NHS
    Trust/Photo Researchers, Inc.,
    80
Victor Habbick Visions, 44, 52,
    57, 88

# ABOUT THE EDITOR

Louise I. Gerdes earned a bachelor's degree in psychology from the University of California, Berkeley, a master's in literature and writing from California State University, San Marcos, and a Juris Doctor from the University of Florida College of Law. Currently she edits educational texts for Greenhaven Press. Areas of distinct interest include biotechnology, the environment, and global justice. She also teaches composition, speech, and critical thinking at the University of Phoenix. She shares a home in Vista, California, with her tuxedo cat, Phineas.